A GUIDE TO THE
OPERA

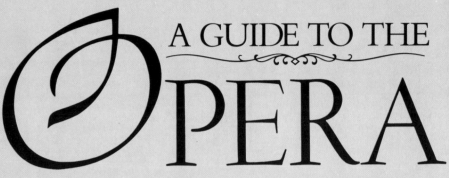

A GUIDE TO THE
OPERA

ROBIN MAY

HAMLYN

For
Jennifer, Michael and Jenny

Photographic acknowledgments

Adelaide Festival Centre 24, 138; Catherine Ashmore, London 11, 14, 20–21, 27, 40, 43, 46–7, 55, 60, 70, 71 top, 73, 80 bottom, 84, 94–95, 98–99, 102–103, 106–107, 118–119, 122, 123 bottom, 131, 132–133, 136–137, 142 bottom; Clive Barda, London 16, 18 top, 21, 23, 26 top, 56, 96, 101, 128, 136, 141 top, 141 bottom; BBC Hutton Picture Library, London 52, 54 top, 90; Zoë Dominic, London 10–11, 12, 16–17, 18–19, 25, 28, 31, 32, 38–39, 40–41, 47, 57, 58–59, 67, 72–73, 74–75, 76–77, 78, 80 top, 81, 82–83, 84–85, 85, 86, 87 top, 92–93, 99, 100, 105, 108–109, 111 bottom, 112 top, 112 bottom, 113, 114–115, 116, 117, 123 top, 125, 132, 134, 134–135, 138–139, 140, 143, 144–145, 146–147, 148; Dominic Photography, London 15, 128–129; Mary Evans Picture Library, London 36 bottom, 42 bottom; Guy Gravett, Hurstpierpoint, Sussex 18 bottom, 33, 34–35, 35, 42 top, 45 bottom, 49 bottom, 50, 137, 149; James Heffernan, New York 65, 126–127; Kent Opera 49 top; Kobal Collection, London 13; © Lelli and Masotti, courtesy of the National Video Corporation Ltd 79; Mansell Collection, London 34, 36 top, 42 top right, 91; MAS, Barcelona 22–23; Robin May Collection, London 29 bottom, 54 bottom, 71 bottom, 87 bottom, 92, 111 top; Andrew Page, London 115; Photo Source, London 29 top; Prince William Yang, Adelaide 26 bottom; Unitel, Munich 30–31, 61, 62, 62–63, 63, 64, 68–69, 88–89, 97, 109, 110, 120–121; Virginia Opera Association, Norfolk, Virginia 148–149; Welsh National Opera, Cardiff 104, 124; Reg Wilson, London 37, 44, 45 top, 48–49, 51, 53, 66–67, 94, 95, 130 top, 130 bottom, 142 top.

Front cover: Placido Domingo and Kiri Te Kanawa in
Manon Lescaut (Zoë Dominic, London)
Back cover: *The Midsummer Marriage* (Zoë Dominic,
London)
Titlespread: *Orpheus in the Underworld* (Catherine Ashmore,
London)

Published by
The Hamlyn Publishing Group Limited
Bridge House, London Road, Twickenham, Middlesex, England

Copyright © The Hamlyn Publishing Group Limited 1987
ISBN 0 600 55292 6

Printed in Spain

CONTENTS

CHAPTER ONE

Ring Up the Curtain

'Bliss was it in that dawn to be alive,' wrote the poet Wordsworth, though, as it happens, he was writing about the French Revolution, not opera. As far as the dedicated opera buff is concerned the cardinal fact about that revolution is that it inspired Giordano to compose his opera *Andrea Chénier*, which is regularly despised in print by critics, but equally regularly enjoyed by opera buffs if the cast is right.

'Bliss' is not an overstatement. From being considered the Cinderella of the arts in critical esteem in many countries, including Britain and America, especially by theatre people, and even somewhat taken for granted in the heartlands of opera, Germany, Italy, Austria, Czechoslovakia and France, opera has suddenly gripped the hearts and minds of millions who had never imagined that opera was for them. There has been nothing like it in

the history of great art since Shakespeare and his contemporaries set Elizabethan and Jacobean England ablaze. True, new operas are not all the rage, but millions around the world are discovering the supreme joys of the old and are even sampling the new. And the new now includes works by Stephen Sondheim (most notably, *Sweeney Todd*) and Andrew Lloyd Webber (*Evita, The Phantom of the Opera*). Opera, which had looked like becoming too advanced for mere mortals, is now ready to embrace Harrison Birtwhistle (*The Mask of Orpheus*) and Thea Musgrave (*Mary, Queen of Scots*), complete with fascinated audiences, as well as past operatic glories. The new no longer automatically alarms.

What has triggered off this explosion? Word of mouth could not do it, for telling those who are suspicious of opera that it is for them is a sterile occupation. Opera conversion often used to be a painfully slow business for those who indulged in such noble work, especially in countries unblessed with enough opera houses. If the potential convert was already a Mozart lover matters became simpler, or if his or her tastes tended towards the Romantic in music, Puccini or Verdi might do the trick. Now things are simpler. Opera is booming and a single word sums up the boom – video. Opera films have, of course, helped, and these appear on television, too, but it is the wealth of video-recorded operas that has created the new excitement.

In the first place it has transformed all but the wealthiest operagoers' lives. In their own living rooms they and those who may be converted can experience La Scala; the Metropolitan Opera, New York; Covent Garden and the English National Opera; the Bolshoi in Moscow; San Francisco's and Chicago's Opera, and the mighty Verona Arena with its 25,000-strong audiences night after night in high summer, where once much grimmer entertainment was available.

Amazing rarities are shown from time to time. The author never expected to live to see a production of Zandonai's *Francesca da Rimini*, but suddenly, one Sunday afternoon, there it was on TV from the Met, sumptuously staged by Franco Zeffirelli, who had been inspired by *art nouveau* for his decor.

Thanks to video newcomers have been drawn to opera, many of whom must have believed that it was not for them – until they experienced it. They have enjoyed Placido Domingo and Kiri Te Kanawa, both ideally cast, in Puccini's youthful fountain of melody, *Manon Lescaut*, and no doubt have also enjoyed recordings of Te Kanawa and José Carreras singing in *West Side Story* and *South Pacific*. One of the greatest operatic basses in history, Ezio Pinza, finally left the operatic stage to star in the latter on Broadway in 1949. Many thousands of potential opera-lovers must have welcomed 1987 in by watching *Die Fledermaus* from Vienna on TV, along with countless operagoers who were already adorers of that enchanting work. They have also been able to enjoy that minor masterpiece of French opera, *Samson et Dalila*, with the magnificent Jon Vickers and the superb Shirley Verrett,

Always entertaining, Saint-Saens' Samson et Dalila *becomes far more than that when great talents are present, in this case, Jon Vickers and Shirley Verrett. The production – with Sidney Nolan's glorious and haunting designs – was first seen at Covent Garden in 1981, conducted by Sir Colin Davis and produced by Elijah Moshinsky. The popular minor classic was transformed into a major artistic experience.*

set against awesomely beautiful designs by the Australian painter Sidney Nolan. The video list is becoming happily large.

There are also the films. Oddly enough, opera films go back to the very early days when Geraldine Farrar, a ranking star of the Metropolitan, portrayed a *silent* film Carmen. That was in 1915, but there were even earlier opera films, the first dating from 1913. Cinema pianists must have had to work overtime, assuming they knew the music.

On the whole the opera films that appeared down the years were for buffs, the best being straight filmed versions of famous stage productions. Notable examples include the Paul Czinner films of two Salzburg productions, *Der Rosenkavalier* and *Don Giovanni*, also the Zeffirelli-Karajan *La Bohème* from La Scala. Then in the 1980s opera films came of age, with three outright masterpieces that have dramatically helped to increase the surge of interest in the art: Joseph Losey's *Don Giovanni*, superbly made in and around the Vicenza area of Italy; Zeffirelli's sumptuous *La Traviata* and Francesco Rosi's *Carmen*, the first and last having Ruggero Raimondi as, respectively, Don Giovanni himself and the toreador Escamillo. In

Franco Zeffirelli's film of La Traviata, *starring Domingo, Teresa Stratas and Cornell MacNeil, is as sumptuous as it is enjoyable. Violetta's house was gigantic, including this ballroom! The beautiful Stratas is an enchanting Violetta.*

Traviata, Teresa Stratas was perfection, and, for newcomers to vocal art, a striking example of a singer who is a dramatic and a coloratura soprano, as Verdi wanted. Raimondi has a beautiful bass voice and a handsome, magnetic presence as the toreador (usually sung by a baritone) and as Don Giovanni. Placido Domingo – Alfredo in *Traviata* and Don José in *Carmen* – is an example of a heroic and a lyric tenor, lyrical especially when he was younger. (Carreras, too, is a lyric tenor with a most beautiful voice and striking looks. To have two such tenors at one time is a blessed and rare bonus for operagoers. To have three – the third being, of course, Luciano Pavarotti – is riches indeed.)

The film of *Otello* is not as fine as the three mentioned above because of cuts and changes made by the director, but Domingo is superb, as are Katia Ricciarelli and Justino Diaz. Yet another bonus in the fight to widen opera's appeal came in the film *Diva*, when Julia Migenes-Johnson, the fiery Carmen of Rosi's film, a superb performance, sang Catalini's best known aria in *La Wally*, a hit tune for millions who were not expecting to like a luscious, full-blown operatic aria.

This surge of interest in opera has finally killed the (to opera lovers) incredible idea that operatic singing is unnatural, let alone the old nonsense that opera itself is unnatural. That it is the hardest of the

ABOVE
Following its premiere in Stuttgart in 1984, Philip Glass's Akhnaten, *set in Ancient Egypt, was staged by Houston Grand Opera later that year and by English National Opera in 1985. It was magnificently produced by David Freeman and conducted by Paul Daniel. Sally Burgess as Nefertiti and counter tenor Christopher Robson as Akhnaten are kneeling.*

RIGHT
As part of the Olympic Arts Festival, the new Covent Garden production of Turandot *had its premiere at Los Angeles in 1984, opening at the Royal Opera House later that year. Sir Colin Davis conducted, the designer was Sally Jacobs and the producer, Andrei Serban.*

performing arts to achieve perfection in is another matter. It asks a lot of its performers and nowadays often gets it.

Video has been the greatest revolution, and the greatest revelation to a huge new audience. In fact the only threat to opera is the sheer expense of staging it, complete with a full symphony orchestra. This is no problem in countries like Italy, Germany and Austria, and most other European countries, which allow opera huge subsidies, but a constant threat in Britain and, especially, America. The problem is lessened on occasion now by co-productions, settings being moved from one house to another – across the world if need be. Internationalism makes for strain as well as fame, however, as those singers in demand fly from place to place. In earlier times a star might stay in one opera house for a whole season. Those days are now gone and there are also record sessions and television appearances.

The sheer mechanics of staging an opera are formidable, whether settings are traditional and realistic, or impressionistic, or somewhere in between. Life backstage in a great opera house can be hectic, especially when, as at Covent Garden, the Royal Opera shares the house with the Royal Ballet. Crises can occur on stage as well as off. The miracle is that they happen so rarely.

The newcomer soon comes to recognize the types of voice, though there are many sub-divisions. These are described in an appendix. All are fairly straight-

Zemlinsky's fascinating
The Birthday of the
Infanta *is a tragic fairy
tale in one act taken from
an Oscar Wilde story. It
was staged at Covent
Garden in 1985 as part
of a Zemlinsky double bill.
The conductor was Colin
Davis and the producer
Adolf Dresen. From left
to right: Celina Lindsley,
(The Infanta of Spain),
Kenneth Riegel (the
Dwarf) and Stafford
Dean (Don Esteban, the
Major Domo).*

forward with the exception perhaps of the bass-baritone. The counter tenor is a rarity and few have the power needed to be heard in a large opera house. One of the few is James Bowman whose power is unusual, and who has been the most convincing Oberon in Benjamin Britten's *A Midsummer Night's Dream*.

This modern masterpiece has been enjoyed by unknown numbers on TV, but perhaps the most striking example of video changing attitudes as well as showing operatic techniques at their most brilliant has been Wagner's *Ring* from his own theatre at Bayreuth, conducted by

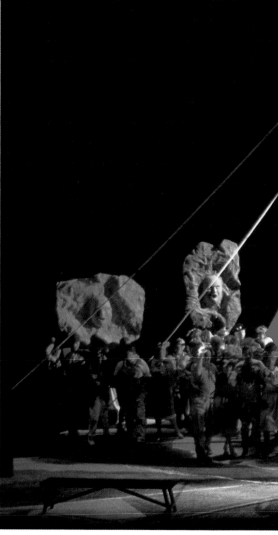

RIGHT
Britten's A Midsummer
Night's Dream *was
produced by Peter Hall at
Glyndebourne in 1981,
with designs by John Bury,
a beautiful production
conducted by Bernard
Haitink. Seen here are
Ileana Cotrubas as
Titania and James
Bowman as Oberon, with
two of the lovers in the
background.*

*Sir Michael Tippett's
The Midsummer
Marriage was first
performed in 1955 at
Covent Garden. A
generation later the
composer has found an
enthusiastic public.
English National Opera's
production in 1985 was
one of a number of
celebrations of the
composer's 80th birthday.
Staged by David Pountney
and designed by Sally
Gardner, it is a brilliant
kaleidoscope of light and
colour. The cast included
Helen Field, Lesley
Garrett, Alfreda
Hodgson, John Treleaven,
Maldwyn Davies and
Anthony Raffell. Mark
Elder was the conductor.*

Pierre Boulez and produced by Patrice Chéreau. It was booed by traditionalists when it was first staged, but is now mainly accepted as a brilliant achievement even if the mixture of visual styles takes some getting used to.

The physical casting was awesomely good, also the standard of acting. Everyone looked his or her part, a remarkable feat in Wagner, whose first essential is a Wagnerian voice. The whole probably gave Wagner the biggest boost since the first festival in 1876.

Almost as striking has been the new sense of adventure sparked off by the video age. Modern operas used to play to empty opera houses – in Britain and America at least – with monotonous regularity. Now, partly perhaps because so many theatregoers have discovered opera, theatre directors included, new territories are being explored in the opera

house. Covent Garden started its 1985–86 season with Stockhausen's *Thursday* from his seven day cycle, *Light*, attracting respectable audiences, then presented a double-bill from Hamburg State Opera of Zemlinsky's *A Florentine Tragedy* and *The Birthday of the Infanta*, both written early in the century, but totally unknown in Britain, the second making quite an impact.

The English National Opera, meanwhile, presented Harrison Birtwhistle's *The Mask of Orpheus*, produced by David Freeman, while Glyndebourne, knowing of course it was on to a good thing, staged George Gershwin's *Porgy and Bess*, produced by Trevor Nunn with an all-black cast. On the opening night Glyndebourne experienced its first standing ovation. Sir Michael Tippett's eightieth birthday was celebrated with a new production of his *The Midsummer Marriage* by Opera

A spectacular view of the most spectacular of all opera 'houses', the Arena di Verona, with Turandot *in progress in 1983.*

North, the composer having lived to see his popularity dramatically increase on both sides of the Atlantic.

The production of the year in Britain in 1986 was Peter Stein's *Otello* for Welsh National Opera. The German director, committed to a touring production, came up with a vision at once simple, inspired, imaginative, theatrical and superbly acted by cast and chorus alike. It was totally true to Verdi's realization of Shakespeare. Richard Armstrong conducted, with seats stripped out of regional theatres to accommodate the orchestra, the result being the surge and thunder of supreme music drama. Jeffrey Lawton was Otello, Helen Field, Desdemona and Donald Maxwell, Iago.

Across the Atlantic Los Angeles Music Center Opera has announced its programmes for 1987–8–9, which are enough to make European opera lovers swoon with the noblest sort of envy. Yet this young organization, with Peter Hemmings, who, with Sir Alexander Gibson, masterminded the rise of Scottish Opera in the 1960s, is following the logical fashion of co-productions from time to time; *La Bohème* from Houston, *The Mikado* with English National Opera and Houston Grand Opera, also *Orpheus in the Underworld* with the same co-presenters. To be noted is Jonathan Miller embarking on *Tristan und Isolde* with Zubin Mehta, designed by David Hockney, a notable trio indeed. Long Beach Opera in

Meanwhile, France has caught opera fever, not for the first time in its history. As well as obvious attractions like Zeffirelli's *Traviata* and Pavarotti in *Bohème* at the Opéra, the Opéra-Comique and Theatre du Châtelet have had mouthwatering attractions, the first including June Anderson and Alfredo Kraus in *La Fille du Régiment* and Britten's *Turn of the Screw*, the second no less than five Rossini operas in a row. Not even the old St. Pancras Festival in London of fond memory ever achieved that. As for Opéra de Lyon staging *Oberon* to celebrate Weber's 200th birthday, and staging it rightly in English, what could be more fine an example of the Entente Cordiale?

The two Germanys are blessed with more opera houses than anywhere else, complete with many premieres each season, including recently a treatment of *Werther, Die Leiden des jungen Werther* at Hamburg by Hans-Jürgen von Bose, and Aribert Reimann's *Troades* from Euripides' *The Trojan Women* at Munich. Janáček's *Osud* (Fate) was in conjunction with English National Opera, while Gelsenkirchen welcomed Birtwhistle's

BELOW
Verdi's Otello *was given a thrilling production by the German theatre director Peter Stein for Welsh National Opera in 1986. He made a virtue of the problems of playing in not very large theatres by concentrating the action – and the audiences' attention – with exceptional skill. Lucio Fanti was the designer. Jeffrey Lawton sang Otello, with Donald Maxwell as Iago and Helen Field as Desdemona. Richard Armstrong conducted. One of the most notable productions of the decade, it is a co-production with the Théâtre Royal de la Monnaie and destined to be seen in Brussels in November 1987.*

California is also a force to be reckoned with, recently presenting the rarely staged Ernst Křenek 1920s jazz opera, *Johnny Strikes Up*, and an ultra-modern version of Mozart's *Seraglio* containing Arab terrorists and a punk, the producer being Christopher Alden. It is well that companies are emerging across the nation and that television opera is booming, for the big three, the Metropolitan, Chicago and San Francisco Operas suffer from the universal shortage of superstars. This increases the importance of the Opera Theater of St. Louis, Virginia Opera, and the Dallas and Washington companies, also Seattle's – a famous Wagner centre, which achieves the possible rather than striving for the impossible.

Punch and Judy. Space forbids real consideration of the vast activity in the two nations, or, indeed, in Italy. La Scala's *Madama Butterfly*, authentically Japanese as directed by Keita Asari, created controversy – and was seen by no doubt millions of Britons on TV, while a highspot in Milan was *Eugene Onegin* in Russian with Mirella Freni in the great role of Tatiana, and Seiji Ozawa as conductor.

All over Italy, far beyond the mighty La Scala and even mightier Verona Arena, opera seasons are to be found, Naples, Rome, Florence and Turin being some of the most famous. Yet so many other opera houses are rich in history, not least Parma's Teatro Regio in the heartland of Verdi country, where singers have been

cheered to the echo, and sometimes been chased to the railway station by a mob, porters refusing to handle their baggage. TV and video have given the world glimpses of La Scala and Verona. Fortunate the opera lover who explores the rest of the country, Sicily included, and can visit that jewel box of a theatre, the Fenice in Venice.

Spain and Sweden have notable seasons of opera, the former's most operatic city being Barcelona. Domingo, Carreras and Caballé need no first names in or out of Spain, while legendary names from the past include Conchita Supervia and Victoria de los Angeles. Another Spaniard, the tenor Alfredo Kraus, is a stylist without equal. The native *zarzuelas* are once

Philip Langridge and Eilene Hannan in Osud, Janáček's autobiographical opera, staged by English National Opera in 1984, produced by David Pountney and conducted by Mark Elder.

A scene from Katiuska, a popular zarzuela by Gonzalez del Castillo and Manuel Alonso with music by Pablo Soro Zabal. This production by the Amadeu Vives Company was seen at the Teatro de la Zarzuela in Madrid.

Janáček's The Makropulos Affair *was staged by the State Opera of South Australia, with Elijah Moshinsky as director and Denis Vaughan as conductor. The lucky audiences experienced the celebrated portrayal by Elisabeth Söderstrom of Emilia Marty, the 300-year-old woman, who does not show her age until the end of the opera.*

again widely enjoyed, having regained the popularity they knew during the 19th century. These ballad operas are essentially national, drawing on folk tales and Spanish literature for plots. Spoken dialogue and folk music contribute to the works which are usually light-hearted. Some of the great Spanish singers learned their stagecraft and polished their vocal talents in this popular form. The Teatro de la Zarzuela has a regular season in Madrid, with a wide range of zarzuelas – and of visiting stars. Most famous singers have appeared at some time in their careers at the Teatro Liceu in Barcelona, which opened in 1847, and was rebuilt after a fire in 1862. Visitors can expect strong casts. The zarzuela performers are in close contact with the audience and sometimes their speeches are improvised. Naturally, knowledge of the language is a

must, though the music is easy on the ear. Even the small Canary Islands have their annual season. There is no end to the spread of opera.

Traditional opera houses abound and are greatly loved, but there are many more modern houses which offer special challenges. When the famous Belgian La Monnaie was being renovated in 1986 its company performed in the Cirque Royal, which proved a splendid venue, works being adapted for new surroundings. José van Dam had a recent triumph there as Verdi's Simon Boccanegra. There is opera in the summer at Puccini's home at Torre del Lago, there is opera on a lake at Bregenz, where singers from the great Vienna State Opera take part. That world-famous house, with its fiercely partisan audience, gets more than its share of crises and has a habit of turning on its artistic

directors at regular intervals. The great Vienna Philharmonic serves the State Opera, while the Volksoper presents operettas and some operas.

The Czechs are particularly devoted to opera and have seen their beloved Janáček become an international favourite in the last decade. Argentina has a famous opera house, the Colón, where German and Italian works are popular. Ireland has some opera, its best known venue being the fabulous Wexford Festival, as miniature a delight as Edinburgh's is huge, though not now very operatic.

Hungary has a fine operatic tradition, Richard Strauss and Klemperer having been among the resident conductors. In Switzerland Zurich is the main operatic centre. Berg's *Lulu* and Hindemith's *Mathis der Maler* had their world premieres there. Berne and Geneva also have

important opera houses. Sweden's operatic capital is Stockholm, its famous singers in the past having included Jenny Lind and Jussi Björling. Birgit Nilsson was the greatest Isolde and Brünnhilde of her generation. There is opera also at Drottningholm, whose charming 18th-century theatre stages 18th-century works each summer.

Russia is almost as famous for its opera as its ballet, and visitors can catch rarities there as well as the supreme masterpieces, *Boris Godunov* and *Eugene Onegin*. Leningrad and Moscow are the key operatic cities, the former with its breathtakingly beautiful Kirov Theatre, the latter with the magnificent Bolshoi. In Moscow, the head of the Lenin Komsomol Theatre, Mark Zakharov, has been responsible for staging *Juno and Avos*, an exciting modern Russian opera with music by Alexei

In 1982 English National Opera presented Ligeti's Le Grande Macabre, *which had its premiere in Stockholm in 1978. This production was conducted by Elgar Howarth and produced by Elijah Moshinsky. John Kane (left) was the White Minister, Roger Bryson (seated), the Black Minister and Marilyn Hill Smith, the Chief of Police.*

Covent Garden revived Peter Hall's 1972 production of Tchaikovsky's Eugene Onegin in 1986. On the left is Neil Rosenshein as Lensky and, on the right, Thomas Allen in the title role. Ileana Cotrubas was Tatiana – a powerful trio indeed.

The Australian Opera's production of Richard Meale's Voss at the Adelaide Festival Theatre, the libretto being taken from Patrick White's novel. The first performance took place at Adelaide in 1986 with Geoffrey Chard and Marilyn Richardson in the leading roles. Jim Sharman was the director with Stuart Challender conducting.

Rybnikov which has been seen in Paris and filmed to be enjoyed internationally.

Sydney, Australia is renowned for its spectacular opera house, though other cities, notably Adelaide and Melbourne, from which Nellie Melba took her name, are operatic centres also. Architecturally world famous, the Sydney Opera House has been greatly aided by the presence of the husband and wife team, conductor and musicologist Richard Bonynge and the great soprano Joan Sutherland. There is an unending line of Australian singers but, happily for Australia, they can now work at home as well as abroad far more than before.

This brief tour of the world of opera has inevitably been representative rather than complete. For instance, Holland, Norway, Poland, Turkey, Rumania, Bulgaria and Yugoslavia have opera houses, as do Mexico, Brazil, Argentina and Uruguay. Brazil can claim one internationally famous composer in Heitor Villa-Lobos (1887–1957). He composed four operas, among them *Izaht* (1940) and one for children, *A Menina das nuvens* (The Little Girl from the Clouds), produced in 1960.

Canada has opera from coast to coast, which has encouraged Canadian singers to return home more frequently. That glorious artist, Jon Vickers, is the most notable of all Canadian singers.

With the development of the long-playing record and jet travel opera singers have achieved international fame. Television and video, as already noted, have helped the process along and the cinema has made a contribution too. Perhaps some singers have been over-idolized but their importance to this most demanding of the performing arts is incalculable. Jon Vickers has been an inspiration to his compatriots. Maria Callas demonstrated that *bel canto* was alive and well – her vocal and dramatic gifts honoured the great Romantic composers and brought their works back to the opera house. A celebrated *Ring*, in English, was made possible because three singers at Sadler's Wells – Rita Hunter, Alberto Remedios and Norman Bailey – came forward under the guidance of Reginald Goodall and proved more than equal to Wagner's demands.

The word 'superstar' is a recent invention, but a very useful one. Opera has

One of the greatest performances of the century, Jon Vickers as Peter Grimes at Covent Garden in 1981. The production by Elijah Moshinsky was first seen in 1975, conducted then and in 1981 by Sir Colin Davis.

27

A few thousand London
operagoers experienced
Callas as Cherubini's
Medea at Covent Garden
in 1959, nights that
instantly became operatic
legend. She is seen here
with the Italian mezzo,
Fiorenza Cossoto.

been blessed – and sometimes cursed – with the breed for centuries, but it was around the turn of the century that the glamorous genre became truly world famous because of the gramophone – the phonograph. This spread the gospel of opera far beyond the opera houses of the world, though much of its music was known through piano arrangements.

The incomparable Enrico Caruso (1873–1921) was not only the operatic superstar of his time, but also *the* recording artist, being the first to sell a million copies of 'Vesti la Giubba' from *I Pagliacci*, though with more than one recording. Nellie Melba, a tough Australian soprano whose actual name was Helen Mitchell, but who took her stage name from Melbourne, near where she had been born, had an outstanding career, especially in French roles. Geraldine Farrar, already noted for her silent films, was a superb Butterfly and Juliette (Gounod), while the Czech soprano Emmy Destinn was superb in both Puccini and Wagner. She was the original Minnie in *La Fanciulla del West* and a fine Elsa and Senta. She was a notable example of the *range* of singers in her day; her Salome was also highly praised. La Scala's choice for the first *Turandot* was Rosa Raïsa, distinguished for, among other roles, her Norma. Another notable Turandot was the Hungarian soprano Maria Nemeth. Her formidable technique enabled her to sing The Queen of the Night in *Die Zauberflöte* as well as Turandot at the Vienna State Opera between the two World Wars. Antonio Scotti was a famous Falstaff and Iago and he often sang with Caruso. He was a notable actor in an age when those who could act did so, while the rest often upset composers by simply singing.

After the Second World War some superb American singers, including the baritones Robert Merrill and Leonard Warren – who died during a performance of *Forza* in 1960 – the soprano Risë Stevens and the tenors Jan Peerce and Richard Tucker, joined the ranks of internationally renowned artists. They followed a great line – the names of Lillian Nordica, Emma Eames and Lawrence Tibbet are part of operatic history. So is that of perhaps the supreme American singer, Rosa Ponselle, whose parents were

ABOVE
In December 1953 the great Norwegian soprano Kirsten Flagstad, internationally renowned as a Wagnerian singer, gave her last concert in Oslo's National Theatre. In 1959 she became Director of the Norwegian National Opera.

LEFT
Caruso was a considerable cartoonist as well as a great singer. Here he is, larger than life, as seen by himself.

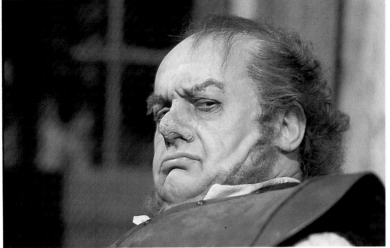

Tito Gobbi as Verdi's Falstaff, one of his most famous roles. The leading Italian baritone of his day, he was very popular in Britain and was closely associated with the Chicago Lyric Theater, as a director as well as a singer.

Italian, a striking looking soprano who sang nineteen seasons at the Met and was an artist who anticipated Callas's triumphs in *bel canto* roles. She has never been forgotten, nor have the triumphs of the English soprano Eva Turner as the definitive Turandot in Italy and elsewhere. The incomparable Wagnerian, Kirsten Flagstad, came to the fore in the 1930s, her successor being the Swedish phenomenon, Birgit Nilsson. The soprano Lotte Lehmann was especially adored and admired for her Marchallin in *Der Rosenkavalier*. The great Italian mezzo, Ebe Stignani, with a voice of remarkable power and purity, enjoyed a career that lasted for thirty-three years. Renata Tebaldi, a golden-voiced soprano, was chosen by Toscanini for the Verdi *Requiem* which re-opened La Scala after the war. She became one of the most admired interpreters of Verdi of her generation. Zinka Milanov, another of Toscanini's choices, made her debut in her native Zagreb in 1927 and retired in 1966, the soprano darling of Met audiences.

The immediate post-war years produced a wealth of singers, many of whom are now legends. There was an Austro-German galaxy that included Elisabeth Schwarzkopf, Lisa della Casa, Hilde Gueden and Dietrich Fischer-Dieskau. Italy's superstars included two idolized heroic tenors, Mario del Monaco and Franco Corelli; Tito Gobbi, the ideal actor-singer, Boris Christoff (born in Bulgaria), a supreme dramatic bass with a tremendous personality; Giuseppe di Stefano, who for some years was a match-

Baritone Dietrich Fischer-Dieskau as Orestes in Götz Friedrich's production of Elektra. *Though principally a lieder singer he has had a distinguished operatic career since his Berlin debut as Rodrigo in* Don Carlos *in 1948. As well as being a leading Wagner and Strauss singer, Fischer-Dieskau is also admired in Verdi roles.*

less lyric tenor, and that most stylish singer, the tenor Carlo Bergonzi, who, at the time of writing, appears to have found the secret of vocal immortality. Above all there was Callas. The double career of Beverly Sills must be mentioned, for this superb *bel canto* singer became Director of the New York City Opera in 1979, adding new lustre to an already legendary career.

There have been sad losses, too, among the post-war ranks. A fine actor-singer, the baritone Ettore Bastianini, died of cancer when he seemed set for glory. Ljuba Welitsch took London and New York by storm, but the Bulgarian soprano's reckless use of her voice brought her career to an early close. Anita Cerquetti was ready to inherit the mantle of Maria Callas – but personal grief persuaded her to withdraw into private life.

There was a post-war event of great importance to opera on the night of 7 January 1955, when Rudolf Bing presented Marian Anderson as Ulrica in *Un Ballo in Maschera* at the Met. The engagement of the celebrated black contralto at a leading house released a stream of hitherto untapped vocal riches; Leontyne Price, Shirley Verrett, Simon Estes, Willard White, and many more took their rightful places in the world's opera houses. Wieland Wagner may be said to have completed the great progression in 1961 when

– not without opposition – he engaged the striking black mezzo, Grace Bumbry, as the Venus for his Bayreuth *Tannhäuser*.

Toscanini ranks as the supreme operatic conductor of the century, his position remaining firm though he died in 1957. Other exceptional conductors, some still in action, include Furtwängler, Fritz Busch, the co-founder of Glyndebourne with Carl Ebert, John Christie and his wife, Audrey Mildmay; Erich – and Carlos – Kleiber, Hans Knappertsbusch, Bruno Walter, Sir Thomas Beecham, who spent a fortune presenting first rate opera in Britain long before the days of subsidies, Victor da Sabata, who inherited Toscanini's mantle at La Scala, Vittorio Gui of Italy and Glyndebourne, Josef Krips, and Rudolph Kempe – to name but a few.

Less glamorous than some, but one who did much to keep the traditions and standards of Italian opera high, was Tullio Serafin, beloved by singers; Maria Callas and Joan Sutherland are just two of those he helped to reach immortality – Callas 'La Divina', the incomparable actress-singer, and Sutherland 'La Stupenda', whose marvel of a voice and engaging personality has delighted audiences for three glorious decades. Yet a fact that needs stressing is that opera at its best depends on every artist.

Opera Is Born

With civil war raging at home, young John Evelyn was very sensibly enjoying himself in Italy. One night in 1645 he went to the opera in Venice. The art had existed for less than fifty years, but the Venetians, who had built the first public opera house in 1637, were so wildly enthusiastic about the new art form that they kept building opera houses.

Evelyn left a valuable account of his evening. He saw a now forgotten piece called *Hercules in Lydia* by Giovanni Rovetta and his description included this splendid summary:

. . . to the Opera, where comedies and other plays are represented in recitative music, by the most excellent musicians, vocal and instrumental, with variety of scenes painted and contrived with no less art of perspective, and machines for flying in the air, and other wonderful notions; taken together, it is one of the most magnificent and expensive diversions the wit of man can invent.

He was very pleased with the singers, who included 'an eunuch', and his 'ears and eyes' were held 'till two in the morning'.

Young operagoers who have experienced early 17th-century operas on stage, television or video will not be surprised by Evelyn's account. Yet as late as the 1950s these operas were scarcely known and very rarely performed indeed. It had been assumed that such works were merely historical monuments. Then came Glyndebourne's famous *L'Incoronazione di Poppea* in 1962 and Monteverdi was revealed to English operagoers as a towering popular genius. *Orfeo*, in Raymond Leppard's realization, was produced by the Sadler's Wells Opera during the following year, and *Poppea* entered the repertory at the Coliseum in 1971. John Eliot Gardiner's realization of *Orfeo*, in an arresting production by David Freeman,

In 1967 Cavalli's L'Ormindo was staged at Glyndebourne, a British 'first', thanks to Raymond Leppard, the conductor editing it from manuscript. Gunther Rennert produced and the cast included Anne Howells, Jane Berbie and John Wakefield, with Hugues Cuénod as the old nurse.

was welcomed by both audiences and critics alike in 1981.

The new art form had been literally invented by a committee, improbable as that may seem. A number of Florentines used to meet in the houses of two noblemen of the city, Jacopi Corsi and Giovanni de'Bardi, the group being known as the Camerata – Society. One of the group was Vincenzo Galilei, father of the astronomer, and another was Jacopi Peri whose *Dafne* is considered to be the first opera.

Naturally, the climate of opinion – the *zeitgeist* – was right for the birth of opera. The Camerata did not inhabit an artistic and intellectual void. When the breakthrough occurred Ancient Greek drama provided the inspiration.

The Camerata wanted words to be more important than music, a challenge to contrapuntal music which so often distorted words. In fact, no one knows exactly how Greek drama was performed, how it sounded, but the Camerata decided that music – a lute, perhaps – should accompany a single voice singing freely, without being obscured by sound that blanketed the words. The first opera, *Dafne*, was staged in 1597, with music by Peri that is lost. Peri's *Euridice* of 1600 survives.

These early efforts paved the way for genius as did the predecessors of Marlowe and Shakespeare in England a few years earlier. That genius was Claudio Monteverdi (1567–1643), whose *Orfeo*, the earliest opera in our repertoire today, dates from 1607. Produced in Mantua, with Alessandro Striggio as librettist, it did for opera what Marlowe's *Tamburlaine the*

Great did for Elizabethan drama, though Marlowe lacked the passionate humanity of Shakespeare and Monteverdi.

When the genius of Monteverdi was revealed in modern times, most notably by Raymond Leppard, the composer's vocal line came as a revelation to those who had assumed that his operas were dull or unperformable or both. He slips naturally from recitative (declamation) through arioso, which is half way between an aria and recitative, to an aria. The resulting music is so masterly and fluid that its expressiveness reveals him as one of the supreme masters, this despite the fact that most of his operas have been lost. How the surviving ones should sound remains controversial. The instruments he had are known and he noted the combinations he wanted for his dazzling tapestry of sound, yet just how it sounded is still a mystery. As for the instruments themselves, a list can be found in Kobbé's *The Complete Opera Book*.

Monteverdi's last opera must rank as one of the greatest in the repertoire and one of the most amoral, for all that its composer was in holy orders in Venice. It is *L'Incoronazione di Poppea* in which evil triumphs decisively over good. Only Verdi amongst Italian composers reached such a pinnacle of greatness, and nothing

The first proscenium arch was at the Teatro Farnese in Parma (1618). A curtain of the Roman type was used. This theatre is not to be confused with the Teatro Regio in Parma with its hugely enthusiastic – or lethal – audiences.

pit – where the stalls are now – sat ordinary folk. Each box had a withdrawing room, which helped to make opera houses social and political centres for leading citizens. These early opera houses were not large. Expansion came in the 18th century.

As the Venetians were very fond of spectacle, cost became a problem – it still is – so casts were often less than eight and the chorus shrank in size. Yet this soon changed because opera's popularity soared. It reached Naples in 1651 and was soon firmly rooted all over Italy. Myths and legends were rivalled as subjects by historical plots, though clarity was often at a discount. One opera – about Hercules – had thirty-three singing parts. Monteverdi had a true successor in Cavalli (1602–76) as Glyndebourne and other audiences know. His *L'Ormindo* and *Calisto* have both triumphed there.

Now opera's centre moved south to Naples and with the move came a change

Glyndebourne's La Calisto *by Cavalli, produced by Peter Hall and designed by John Bury for the 1970 production. The amazing Hugues Cuénod was Linfea and Janet Hughes a convincing faun named Satirino. This was a very enjoyable discovery for artists and audiences alike.*

approaches it until the coming of Mozart. At the end of the opera Monteverdi gives to the evil pair, Nero and Poppea, the first great love duet in opera's history.

The first public opera house, the Teatro San Cassiano, in Venice, opened in 1637, before which audiences tended to be made up of select groups of the nobility and clergy. The new venture was a great success and by 1700 the city had sixteen, with all classes flocking to enjoy great art, as the Elizabethans did, a rare phenomenon in artistic history. It helped that Italy led the world in theatre and stage design. In 1618 the Teatro Farnese in Parma was given the first proscenium arch – with the resulting picture frame effect – which would dominate stage and theatre design until the last quarter of our century saw something of a return to the ideas of the Elizabethans and Greeks before them. Opera by its nature will not desert the proscenium arch.

The scenic effects in Parma and elsewhere were often astounding, stage engineering reaching amazing heights of ingenuity – moving seas and celestial chariots descending from above being regular marvels. The rich occupied boxes and – if they wanted to – followed the libretto by candlelight. Below them in the

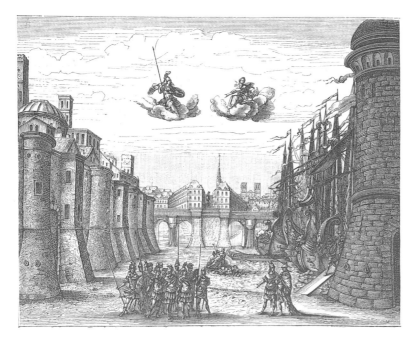

in emphasis. The voice became too important for opera's good, turning opera into a paradise for 'canary-fanciers' performing in virtual 'concerts in costume'. Theatrical truth, always the desire of great operatic composers, was lost, but as will be seen, it would return and return again, despite lapses.

France established an operatic reputation during the 17th century, though more significant was its development of the opera-ballet and, especially, the art of classical ballet. In 1581 an entertainment called *Le Ballet Comique de la Royne* was staged for a royal wedding. It combined music, spectacle, dance, mime and singing. An Italian directed this spectacle, but it was the elevation of an Italian, Mazarin, to become first a Cardinal of France, then its Prime Minister, that helped to make France a power base for gifted Italian theatre folk. The great scenic-artist and stage engineer, Giacomo Torelli, was summoned from Venice and, most importantly, a fourteen-year-old boy named Jean-Baptiste Lully (1632–87) moved from his birthplace Florence to Paris in the suite of the Chèvalier de Guise and rapidly rose to become a power in the land. A composer, dancer, intriguer, violinist and courtier, he became Louis's master of court music, composing opera-ballets and other music and collaborating with Molière. With the poet Philippe Quinault he composed twenty operas, while taking over the new Académie Royale de Musique, founded in 1669, when it was in trouble. He was now operatic dictator of Paris.

Lully and Quinault decided to use mythological or pastoral themes taken from medieval tales of chivalry for their operas at a time when the Italians were using historical characters. Lully's 'airs', as the French called *arias*, were tuneful and simple, while his recitatives used French brilliantly. 'French Overtures' got King and courtiers to their seats, then an allegro announced the glories were on the way. Sadly, Lully died at the height of his fame from an abscess which appeared after he hit his foot instead of the floor with the staff that he used for timekeeping.

His greatest successor was Jean-Philippe Rameau (1683–1764). Not until he was fifty did he make his name as an

opera composer with *Hippolyte et Aricie* in 1733, though the reception was a mixed one. There followed real triumphs with *Les Indes Galantes, Castor et Pollux* and *Zoroastre.* He ranks as the father of modern harmony, a composer who, at his best equalled Bach and Handel and, let it be stressed, is entertaining to listen to. Thanks to him French opera became more dramatic, though by the mid 18th century the light-hearted Italian *opera buffe* were all the rage.

The English have never been so devoted to music as they were in Elizabethan and Jacobean times, certainly not until the 1940s. They sang part songs and solo melodies, the nearest to opera being the Court Masques in Jacobean times, some designed by Inigo Jones the architect who had visited Italy. Ben Jonson, the playwright, often produced these entertainments which were a blend of song, dance and acting. In fact, the Jacobean masques were an English form of opera-ballet.

Born about 1659, Henry Purcell wrote much incidental music for plays, some of which were semi-operatic, though the principals spoke. Not so in *Dido and Aeneas,* the first true English opera (1689 or 1690). It lasts an hour and it was first performed by girls of the Chelsea school run by Josias Priest. Finely constructed, it is musically enchanting, and 'When I am laid in earth', Dido's glorious lament, and the final chorus which follows it, are opera at their finest. Purcell died in 1695 and it would be more than 250 years before another truly great opera would be written by a British composer, *Peter Grimes* by Benjamin Britten.

In 1710 one of the supreme masters of music arrived in England, but alas, except in his own time, few have considered him as a master of opera – of music drama. George Frederick Handel, born in 1685,

was destined to be loved by the British more than any other serious composer. It was no fault of his that he overwhelmed native talent and triggered off a daunting line of second-rate oratorios. As for his operas, much admired in their day, and rich in glorious music, they lack sustained drama, musically as well as dramatically. They also lack those unfortunate phenomena, the *castrati*, eunuchs whose vocal powers were astounding, their voices having volume, flexibility and range. These operatic superstars were used by Monteverdi and only faded out in the 1820s, though the Vatican used them even later.

Naturally, there is much musical pleasure to be had in a Handel opera but,

ironically, some of his oratorios – *Samson*, especially – make better operas than his own. It did not help that the *da capo* aria, an essentially unoperatic form, was all the rage. It contains two parts, the first being repeated with musical ornaments, upon which the singer was obliged to leave the stage. The librettos were mainly uninspired, and trios and quartets were in short supply. Tunes of glory there were in abundance.

Born in Halle in Germany, Handel first made his name in Hamburg. He also worked in Italy, but London gave him true fame from 1711, when his *Rinaldo* was heard. His successes included *Radamisto*, *Giulio Cesare* (with a castrato hero), *Tamerlano* and *Rodelinda*. The

its own day could it really bite, but it still holds the stage with its mockery of operatic conventions, bad librettos and contrived happy endings, plus rivalries between singers. Politicians were also attacked, especially the prime minister, Sir Robert Walpole, the hero Macheath being in part a satire on him. There were scores of other ballad operas, plays with music rather than light operas, the composer of *Rule Britannia!*, Thomas Arne, contributing *Thomas and Sally* and *Love in a Village* in the 1760s, and Sheridan, author of *The School for Scandal*, writing *The Duenna* (1775), with his father-in-law, Thomas Linley, compiling and composing the music. These were operatic lightweights compared with the typical *opera seria* of the century which even Handel could not bring to operatic life. Opera needed the genius of the young Mozart to provide the vital spark that was needed to bring life to the ponderous form.

It was a form that bred a type of operagoer not extinct today, the canary-fancier, whose only interest is the voice supplying suitable song. The mythological or heroic plots were as tortuous as the formality of the structure and the music of the operas were rigid – and totally out of touch with life. Audiences sitting in the undarkened theatres of the day talked while waiting for arias, so were often provided with a string of arias called a *pasticcio* – a pie – to keep them happy. Naples, alas, was notorious for such feats, but was also the centre of a true form of art, the *opera buffa*.

Comedy in opera stems back to Monteverdi, but Neapolitans decided to add whole scenes of it to the end of acts. So popular were they that some became comic pieces – intermezzi – in their own right, which were staged between acts, and which paved the way for Rossini. Dialogue was sung in recitative, which got the plot across melodically and efficiently – and operatically. *Opera seria* had neglected duets and ensembles: *opera buffa* thrived on them, also on the exuberant, indeed fizzing, finales.

Better still, the *opera buffe* were in touch with ordinary people, their hopes and fears, loves and lusts. The plays of Carlo Goldoni and Carlo Gozzi were plundered

LEFT
English National Opera's production of Handel's Xerxes in 1985 with Ann Murray and Rodney Macann (kneeling), staged by Nicholas Hytner and conducted by Sir Charles Mackerras. Also in the cast was Valerie Masterson as a striking Romilda.

1730s saw *Alcina* and *Serse*, both revived in modern times, the latter starting with an aria that became – quite wrongly – a quasi-religious classical 'pop', Handel's *Largo*, a languid piece, not a holy one. His switch to oratorios was due to intrigues and the hostility of certain composers and singers – and to the runaway success of *The Beggar's Opera* in 1728. England's musical darling he may have been, but he had more than his share of enemies. His truly English work is the lovely pastoral, *Acis and Galatea*.

The Beggar's Opera has a place in musical and theatrical history. The text was by John Gay, the music assembled by John Christopher Pepusch from popular ballads, who added music of his own. Only in

example of late *opera buffa*. So pleased was Emperor Leopold II of Austria by it at its premiere in Vienna in 1792 that he gave the cast supper before having them perform it again.

For historical importance Cimarosa's opera yields pride of place to Pergolesi's, for in 1746, ten years after his death, his *opera buffa* was staged in Paris by an Italian troupe.

La Serva Padrona shook the French musical establishment. Supporters of the Italian school attacked Rameau, now an old man, the chief attacker being the philosopher, Jean-Jacques Rousseau. He proclaimed that only Neapolitan opera was worth listening to and even wrote one of his own, *Le Devin du Village* (1752), 'devin' being a sage. He and others made

Paul Jones and Belinda Sinclair in the National Theatre's production of The Beggar's Opera *in 1983. Both theatre and opera companies have staged it down the years.*

for plots, and stock characters of the old improvised *commedia dell' arte* routine – Arlecchino, Pulcinella, Pantalone and the rest – were conscripted into operas. Pergolesi's *La Serva Padrona* (The Maid Mistress), first seen in Naples in 1733 as an intermezzo in his *Il Prigonier Superbo*, was the most famous early example of the genre. In it a servant girl lures her master into marriage, its third character being a mute. The composer of this sparkling piece died in his mid-twenties. Many *opera buffe* were written in the local dialect, making them even more popular. Most famous of all was Niccolo Piccini's *La Buona Figliuola* (The Good Daughter), first staged in 1760. There is feeling as well as humour in the piece, anticipating Mozart rather than Rossini.

Better known than either is *Il Matrimonio Segreto*, by Domenico Cimarosa based on *The Clandestine Marriage* by George Colman and David Garrick. This still holds the stage and is a fine *opéra comique* an essentially French art form. It must be stressed that it did not have to be comic, but was a mixture of song and dialogue. That sublimely serious opera *Fidelio* is an *opéra comique* by French reckoning. The two masters of the form in the later 18th century were François Philidor and the Belgian André Grétry, whose *Zémire et Azore* is still performed.

The battle between Italians and French was mainly fought between 1752 and 1754, with the Italian's adherents winning because their imported product was so high-spirited and life-enhancing. In the event *opéra comique* would be more realistic than *opera buffa*, neither better nor worse but different.

And where was that very opera-minded nation Germany at this time? Its king-doms, duchies etc. were musically dominated by Italians or Italian-inspired native composers, though Reinhardt Keiser and Georg Telemann had written German operas before the Italian conquest. The *singspiel*, a similar genre to the English ballad opera and the French *opéra comique*, challenged the foreigners in the 1750s. Joseph Haydn (1732–1809) wrote operas for his employer at Esterhazy Castle, fifteen of which survive, more Italian rather than German. His operas are not in the regular repertoire, *Il Monda della Luna* (The World on the Moon) from a play by Goldoni, being the most performed. However, there was one great German-born master of opera – and a reformer of it – a genius named Christoph Willibald von Gluck.

Handel's Semele, *one of his most delightful operas, was produced at Covent Garden in 1982 by John Copley with Sir Charles Mackerras conducting. Valerie Masterson was a splendid Semele.*

Like Willy Loman in Arthur Miller's *Death of a Salesman*, Gluck is 'liked, but he's not – well-liked'. Even his finest operas, though given from time to time, are not regularly staged for he had no great melodic gift. Yet he was a great reformer, and if it is true that some of his finest inspirations came to him when seated in a field at his piano, a bottle of champagne on each side of him, then he was a genial eccentric as well as an important operatic master.

His first opera, *Artaserse* (1741), was an *opera seria*, with a libretto by Metastasio, the busiest librettist of the day, but after settling in Vienna he began to rebel against the genre. Though he spent some twenty years or more before he was able to cast aside current conventions – years of composing conventional Italian operas – he was preparing himself for his first great work. It was another Italian opera – he never wrote a German one – but this was a masterpiece, *Orfeo ed Euridice* (1762). His librettist, the poet Raniero da Calzabigi, was another reformer.

Gluck's two most popular pieces come from the opera, Orfeo's incomparable 'Che faro senza Euridice?' (What is life without Euridice?) and 'The Dance of

In 1982 Dame Janet Baker's glorious career in opera ended at Glyndebourne, where she sang the title role in Gluck's Orfeo ed Euridice, *produced by Peter Hall. John Bury was the designer and Raymond Leppard conducted.*

Il Matrimonio Segreto *by Cimarosa, from George Colman's play,* The Secret Marriage, *was staged at Glyndebourne in 1965 with Albertina Valentini, Rosa Laghezza, Federico Davià and Carlo Badioli.*

Christoph Gluck, the great German composer, was one of opera's reformers, who sought musical and dramatic truth. Some of his greatest feats were achieved, it is said, when at a piano in a field with a bottle of champagne on each side of him. His best-known work is Orfeo ed Euridice *(1762, revised for Paris 1774).*

The magic picture from the opera Zémire et Azor *(1771). André Grétry's best-known work, it is a version of the story of Beauty and the Beast. Grétry was a master of opéra comique.*

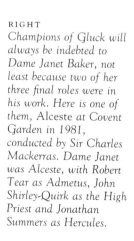

Blessed Spirits'. He had now found the 'beautiful simplicity' he had searched for. He used accompanied recitative, limited the power of his singers, and unleashed deep human emotions, which had been absent for too long from opera. A castrato sang the title role, but Gluck rewrote it for a tenor in Paris. The most famous interpreters have been Pauline Viardot in Paris in 1859 and Kathleen Ferrier in 1952 at Covent Garden, an overwhelming performance by a dying woman.

In 1767 came *Alceste*, with a preface that called for music which served poetry and with singers in second place. *Paride et Elena* and *Iphigénie en Aulide* followed, the second a French opera, as was the less successful *Armide*. Now an impresario commissioned both Gluck and Niccolo Piccini to write *Iphigénie en Tauride*. The latter was now following Gluck's ideas, but was outclassed by a masterpiece. *Echo et Narcisse* failed the same year, 1779, and Gluck virtually retired.

The operagoer, like other lovers of the arts, is well aware that the greatest art is miraculous, and the short life of Mozart provides an outstanding example of the miracle. Born in 1756, Wolfgang Amadeus Mozart poured much of his most personal music into his operas. Fortunately for posterity, he grew up when the symphony orchestra – though it would acquire later additions – had achieved maturity. As well as his matchless musical talent, he had true theatrical flair and for three of his supreme masterpieces he had a marvel of a librettist in Lorenzo da Ponte, a Casanova-like character who helped establish opera in New York, where he died at the age of 89.

Like Shakespeare – to whom he was compared by Goethe – Mozart was not a revolutionary. Heroes and devils are not the characters of his operas, but real people. Like Shakespeare, Mozart (and the librettist Da Ponte) was ambivalent, artistically neutral but with boundless sympathy for his creations. Beethoven was puritanically shocked by *Don Giovanni* and even *The Marriage of Figaro*.

Mozart's father Leopold was Kapellmeister to the Archbishop of Salzburg. That the boy was the ultimate musical prodigy does not mean that his early music, operas included, are masterpieces, but they are significant. His first opera, *La Finta Semplice* (The Simple Prince), was written at the age of eleven at the suggestion of the Emperor of Austria, who specified an Italian one. It was staged at Salzburg in 1769. *Bastien et Bastienne* followed, which had a German libretto, then came a triumph in Milan with *Mitridate, Re di Ponto* in 1770, Mozart conducting the opera from the piano (some composers played first violin). Also premiered in Milan were *Ascanio in Alba* and *Lucia Sillo*, respectively in 1771 and 1772, the latter showing portents of things to come.

In 1775 Munich welcomed *La Finta Giardiniera* (The Disguised Gardener's Girl), which had sharper characterization than his earlier works, while the same year

saw *Il Re Pastore*, little more than a succession of arias. *Zaide* in 1779 was far finer, though unfinished. It is a singspiel, a German form of ballad opera, developed in the 18th century, and was a taste of masterpieces to follow. The first great Mozart opera, *Idomeneo*, triumphed in Munich in 1781, but though it was performed after his death, it virtually vanished until given again in Germany between the wars. This passionate *opera seria* enriched and transcended the dying genre, the result being a true music drama.

Die Entführung aus dem Serail (The Abduction from the Seraglio) is a youthful and joyously unsophisticated singspiel, a marvellous musical play with spoken dialogue, and it is greatly loved.

There followed two minor pieces, then a pleasant comedy, *Der Schauspieldirecktor*, (The Impresario), set in the world of opera. Then came maturity, and the full flowering of his genius. The year was 1786, the opera, *Le Nozze de Figaro*, based on Beaumarchais' play which had created a sensation in Vienna as well as France, the Emperor finding it far too revolutionary. One speech by Figaro, poor writer turned valet-barber, challenged the Count directly about the nobility ruling through privilege of birth. Mozart, anxious to turn the work into an opera, persuaded the dissolute Abbé Lorenzo da Ponte to provide a libretto, implying, rather than stating the criticism of the nobility. Antonio Salieri, the leader of Vienna's Italian musicians, hoped for a failure, but had to endure a major success,

though it was the performances at Prague that really established the work's fame. 'Here they talk about nothing but *Figaro*,' wrote Mozart. 'Nothing is played, sung or whistled but *Figaro*.'

Perfection is not easy to describe. How concisely Mozart portrays a youth discovering the joys of love and sex in Cherubino's 'Non so piu'; how brilliantly he brings the tiny part of Barbarina to life

in her lament for a lost pin. It is a deeply moving work for all its high spirits. Rosina is not here the cheerful girl of Rossini's *The Barber of Seville*, though she takes her part in the comedy scenes. Ultimately she lives for us in two great and serious arias, 'Porgi amor' and 'Dove sono?'

The opera's pace is remarkable, and if dramatic tension slips a little in the last act, characterization is deepened, as in Figaro's jealous aria when he thinks that his Susanna has betrayed him. At the end the arrogance of the Count ends and he asks his wife's forgiveness, a deeply charged moment before a radiant finale.

Next came *Don Giovanni* in 1787, premiered in Prague with overwhelming success. It took the Viennese longer to respond to it; even the Emperor, who admired it, telling Mozart that 'such music is not meat for the teeth of my Viennese'. 'Give them time to devour it,' said the composer, and they did. It is and has been much argued over. The Romantic Movement resulted in its tragic side being stressed, the curtain coming down with the Don's descent into hell. Da Ponte, however, called it a *dramma giocoso*, a gay drama in the traditional sense of the adjective. Mozart mixes tragedy and comedy so skilfully that the comedy becomes sublime, while the power of the final scene when the statue comes to take possession of the Don has Mozart reaching new heights of power.

ABOVE
Kiri Te Kanawa as the Countess in Covent Garden's 1971 production of Mozart's Le Nozze di Figaro. *On the left is Patricia Kern as Cherubino, on the right, Reri Grist as Susanna.*

LEFT
A notable production of Don Giovanni *opened in Cardiff in 1984. The guest producer of the Welsh National Opera was Ruth Berghaus from the German Democratic Republic, renowned throughout Europe for her work. She aimed to show a world on the knife-edge between the old and new regimes. The Don was played by William Shimell, who has gone down to hell just before the scene pictured here. The cast from left to right: Laurence Dale as Ottavio, Jonathan Best as Masetto, Anne Evans (at the back) as Donna Anna, Elaine Woods as Elvira, Beverley Mills as Zerlina and Nicholas Folwell as Leporello. Sir Charles Mackerras conducted.*

Così fan tutte (1790) means 'Thus do they all', meaning all women. The plot is said to be true and concerns two lovers who apparently go away, but return disguised as Albanians to test the fidelity of their sweethearts. Da Ponte again provided the libretto. It is a thin story, though neat enough, with the two pairs of lovers, the delightful maid Despina, and the sophisticated Don Alfonso. For some, Mozart never wrote a more ravishing score than this. The situation is farcically funny but can be ruined by arch acting. It is also a serious work, some have claimed a disturbing one, though fundamentally it is sheer enchantment.

Mozart's last great masterpiece, *Die Zauberflöte* (The Magic Flute), was first

performed in 1791, the year he died. Its libretto was the work of Emanuel Schikaneder, in whose Theater auf der Wieden in Vienna it was first staged, with Schikaneder as the first Papageno.

The Magic Flute, a mixture of sublime melodies, fantasy, Masonic ritual and humour, and his own spiritual and religious aspirations, has always been greatly

loved, and some credit must be given to Schikaneder. The last words on it must be Wagner's: 'Before it German opera scarcely existed: this was the moment of its creation.'

In the same year Mozart's *opera seria*, *La Clemenza di Tito*, was staged in Prague. It cannot be considered as successful an *opera seria* as *Idomeneo*, but a fine

49

Mozart's Die Zauberflöte (The Magic Flute) was produced at Glyndebourne in 1978 by John Cox with David Hockney's brilliant, and totally successful, designs and costumes.

Mozartian cast can make it blaze and convince some that it is a masterpiece. Mozart's early death is a source of endless comment and eternal regret. What would he have achieved if he had been spared for just five more years – or forty-five? As it is his legacy is incomparable and, with Verdi and Wagner, he ranks as the ultimate justification for the art of opera.

Mozart's successor found *Don Giovanni* and even *The Marriage of Figaro* 'repugnant' and 'too frivolous', for Beethoven had very high ideals. He naturally preferred *The Magic Flute*. His one opera, *Fidelio*, reflects his outlook, and it took him far longer to write than Mozart took to compose his operas. For Beethoven, composition was painstakingly slow. *Fidelio* has four overtures, the three *Leonoras* and the final *Fidelio* overture that is used. The story, said to be true, has a wife dressing in male clothes to rescue her husband, a political prisoner, from prison.

It is a good melodramatic plot and Beethoven, stirred by the theme, wrote a masterpiece. First given in 1805 in Vienna, the final revised version dates from 1814. It starts as a singspiel and ends as deeply emotional music drama, a sublime masterpiece. The light opening gives no indication that a peak of emotion will be reached in the first act with an overwhelming Prisoners' Chorus, while the first scene of the second and last act has the hero Florestan rescued from his dungeon by his wife, disguised as a young man. A merely good composer would have provided excitement: Beethoven provides that, plus sublimity. The final scene, with all the prisoners freed, is radiantly, exultantly joyous. Darkness and light, freedom and imprisonment, justice and injustice, are high themes. Beethoven, the link between Classic and Romantic for those who like labels, was the ideal composer for such a timeless story.

CHAPTER THREE

From Weber to Wagner

The Romantic Movement

Artistic labels are useful but should be treated with suspicion. Why should a Mozart lover be told that his idol wrote 'classical' music, whereas Berlioz was a Romantic? Yet labels are useful. The Romantics exploited their feelings more emotionally, subjectively and passionately than their predecessors in the arts.

More than anywhere else, Paris was the birthplace of Romanticism. Musically it branched off into German and Italian tributaries, which produced, respectively, two overwhelming talents in Wagner and Verdi. These two will be described in this and the next chapter before returning to France where so many great musicians settled in its capital.

The creator of the German school of opera was Carl Maria von Weber. Before

the glorious night when history was made, Weber, born in 1786, had composed several operas including *Peter Schmoll* and the lively *Abu Hassan*. Later he would write that 'all Germans' wanted 'a self-contained work of art', one in which all the arts would work together, vanish, then appear once more to found a new world. His masterpiece, *Der Freischütz*, would do just that. It means 'the free-shooter', one who shoots magic bullets, and its premiere in Berlin on 18 June 1821, was greeted ecstatically. The excitement continued wherever it was performed in Germany. Just as Verdi would help unite Italy before political unity was achieved, so Weber united Germany with this tuneful Romantic score. Outside Germany the opera is perhaps rather patronizingly enjoyed, but for Germans it is a seminal part

BELOW
With his Der Freischütz *Weber founded and inspired German Romantic opera – and greatly influenced the young Richard Wagner. In Covent Garden's 1977 production René Kollo sang the hero, Max, Hannelore Bode was Agathe, Lucia Popp, Aennchen, and Kurt Moll, Caspar.*

of their birthright. Folk-songs vie with superb arias, the most famous scene being set in the Wolf's Glen where Kaspar, having sold his soul to the evil spirit Samiel, makes magic bullets for the huntsman hero Max. The scene is splendid; fine atmospheric musical melodrama. The magnificent overture made history, for its opening evokes the German forests which Wagner would later immortalize.

Musically, *Euryanthe* (1823) was another marvel, but its story is dire. Unlike *Der Freischütz*, it has no spoken dialogue, but it has a number of dramatic recitatives. Poor Weber's health broke down and *Der Freischütz* made fortunes for others, not him. In 1824, however, he was asked to write an opera for Covent Garden. The result was *Oberon*, a fairy tale set to superb romantic music. There is much spoken dialogue, creating problems for most singers. Weber died soon after the premiere. Twenty years later his body was returned to Germany and buried in Dresden. Among the mourners was Richard Wagner.

In the early years of this century, many who considered themselves musical in Anglo-Saxon countries only acknowledged German operas. A curious thing about this cult was that it was based on a very limited repertoire. As will be seen, there were a number of fine composers of

the second rank, but the standard repertoire in much of the operatic world outside Germany and Austria has for many years only contained a handful of examples of German operatic art: *Fidelio*, most of Wagner, *Hänsel und Gretel* by Humperdinck, and perhaps Flotow's *Martha*.

Clearly the chief reason for this is that certain major German composers either failed as opera composers or avoided it, except as conductors or listeners, namely Brahms, Bruckner and Mahler. Weber, of course, did not fail, but even his epochmaking *Der Freischütz* is not truly a part of the standard repertoire except in central Europe. However, as visitors to Germany and Austria know, there are many most enjoyable works of the second rank that are constantly staged in both Germany and in Austria, not simply because there are over a hundred opera houses in lyrical action.

The works of Franz Schubert (1797–1828) are rarely to be found for the very basic reason that none are truly stageworthy. Of his ten operas, some uncompleted or lost, and five operettas the least lost cause is *Die Verschworenen* (The Conspirators, 1823), a Lysystrata comedy retitled *Der Häusliche Krieg* (The Domestic War). With such a supreme lyrical gift it is surely certain that he would have achieved a success if he had lived

Dresden was the birthplace of opera in Germany. Illustrated is its famous opera house in 1888. It was bombed in the Second World War but was restored to be exactly as it had been before, being reopened in 1985. Wagner's Rienzi, Der Fliegende Höllander *and* Tannhäuser *were all premiered at Dresden.*

longer. Mendelssohn failed also, while Robert Schumann's one opera, *Genoveva*, suffered from a bad libretto and is far less effective than many of the Italian works that he so disparaged.

Fortunately, lesser composers achieved finer operas. Ludwig Spohr's *Faust* (1816) has been claimed as the first Romantic opera, and *Zémire und Azor* and *Jessonda* are two of his other successes. He was also one of the first conductors in the modern sense and was an early champion of Wagner. Heinrich Marschner (1795–1861) was a leading Romantic, *Der Vampyr* and his masterpiece *Hans Heiling* being two other notable works. Albert Lortzing (1801–51) is a little better known outside Germany, where he is greatly loved; *Zar und Zimmermann* (Tsar and Carpenter) and *Der Wildschütz* (The Poacher) are his most famous operas. Lortzing's career is a reminder of how difficult life was before proper copyright laws were introduced. As it was, the composer, who was also a singer, librettist and conductor and orchestral player, could never concentrate solely on composition. He is still loved in Germany for his true Romantic feeling. *Zar und Zimmermann* is a jolly piece about Peter the Great when he was working in Holland as a carpenter, while *Der Wildschütz* is his masterpiece. He died in poverty in Berlin where he was conductor at a small theatre

and about to lose his post, this at a time when his operas were triumphing all over Germany.

Friedrich von Flotow (1812–83) is better known outside Germany because of one opera, despised by the sort of critic who will not allow the right of good second-rate operas of considerable melodic charm to exist. The opera in question is *Martha* (1847). Set in Queen Anne's England, it is a romantic comedy in which two ladies, disguised as servants, are hired by two farmers. It is a delightful minor work which uses the old Irish melody 'The Last Rose of Summer' to great effect, and which has one superb aria, 'M'appari', ('Ach, so Fromm' in the original), which generations of tenors and audiences have taken to their hearts. Sadly it is seldom performed today.

Otto Nicolai (1810–49) is also remembered by one opera, *Die lustigen Weiber von Windsor* (1849) based on Shakespeare's *Merry Wives*. That Verdi later surpassed it, and even excelled Shakespeare, does not alter the earlier work's charm, though only its famous overture is well known outside Germany. But now there was a colossus on the scene, whose influence ranged far beyond the world of opera, and who even now, a century after his death, remains controversial and the most extraordinary figure in operatic history.

Flotow's Martha *is a charming piece with one hit tune, 'M'appari', and with much use of 'The Last Rose of Summer'. When staged by Sadler's Wells Opera in the 1950s audiences purred and the critics sneered.*

The exterior of the theatre at Bayreuth just before it was opened for the first performances of Wagner's Ring cycle in 1876. It was the culmination of years of hope, anguish, despair and more hope.

RIGHT
Richard Wagner (1813–83), composer, librettist, conductor, producer, polemicist, titanic genius.

Richard Wagner was born in Leipzig in 1813, the same year as that less controversial genius Verdi. No composer has had such artistically boundless a vision as Wagner, who lived to achieve his ambitions. Listing his faults as a man is pointless. Without ruthlessness, iron determination and luck he could never have created and staged *Der Ring des Nibelungen*, the most colossal work of art in the history of music drama.

Wagner set out to produce a *Gesamtkunstwerk*, unifying the arts into his own style of music drama. He of course did not invent music drama: Monteverdi for one was undoubtedly creating them. Yet the phrase came to be widely used because of him, his desire to unite the musical and dramatic features in a work as never before and curtail the prominence of singers (though still writing monumentally for them). Verdi, too, would write music dramas, but as a true Italian he never curtailed the voice.

Visually, he never achieved his ends for in his day German scenic art was second rate, but it is wrong to criticize his stage effects for being over-ambitious. The straight theatre of his day could stage train crashes, horse races, etc., far more complex effects than a mounted lady warrior or a dragon. He was an inspired director of acting, but when he died in 1883 his admittedly gifted widow Cosima fossilized his productions despite strong objections by leading theatre designers, most notably Adolphe Appia. Not until his grandsons Wieland and Wolfgang took over the theatre and Festival after the Second World War did Bayreuth become a major centre of music drama as its founder had tried to make it.

Inevitably, Wagner's contemporaries thought of him as a revolutionary, which he was, but he was not an iconoclast for his roots lay deep in German music, in the work of Mozart, Weber and especially Beethoven, whose Choral Symphony was a stepping stone to his own mighty works.

He was very much a man of the theatre. Like all major opera composers he is known to have keenly wanted singers who could act, indeed a turning point in his life was Wilhelmine Schröder-Devrient's Leonore in *Fidelio*. He was electrified and saw what a great artist could achieve by interpreting a masterpiece dramatically as well as musically.

In rehearsal: Simon Estes as the Flying Dutchman and Robert Lloyd as Daland in Mike Ashman's controversial production of Wagner's early masterpiece at Covent Garden in 1986. Rosalind Plowright was Senta and Siegfried Jerusalem, Erik.

Wagner's first success, Rienzi, was given a rousing production by English National Opera in 1983, the work being updated to the days of Hitler and Mussolini, complete with the use of film. Cheers and boos greeted the production, the first being correct because the transposition worked. From left to right: Kathryn Harries as Irene, Kenneth Woollam as Rienzi and Felicity Palmer as Adriano.

He so admired 'The Queen of Tears' as she was known that she was the first Adriano in Rienzi, Senta in Der Fleigende Holländer (The Flying Dutchman) and Venus in Tannhäuser, despite the fact that her technique was imperfect and her voice had lost its top notes early in her career.

Wagner did not invent the leitmotiv, though no one has ever used 'leading motives' so melodically, subtly and organically than he. The operas can be enjoyed without knowing any of their names – the Sword motif and the rest – but they do help when following the music dramas. The librettos, too, deserve study. Wagner never believed that all that matters is the music.

Only a minority of Wagnerites are born. The rest start with boredom relieved by highspots. The invention of the long-playing record and, later, the video cassette has hastened the process of reaching Valhalla considerably. Gradually the

operas are absorbed, while Wagner's endings are so stupendous that even the most weary is invigorated.

Originally Wagner thought of being an actor, but by 1833 he was chorus master at the Würzburg Opera. The small company gave him good experience. He wrote Die Feen (The Fairies) there, though it was not staged in his lifetime. Neither it nor Das Liebesverbot (Love's Denial), based on Shakespeare's Measure for Measure, showed signs of coming greatness.

In 1836 Wagner married Minna Planer, an actress who was too conventional to cope with him, though at this time Wagner was a pleasant enough young professional. The iron had not yet entered into his soul, iron that would sustain him in titanic battles ahead. The Wagners went to Königsberg, then Riga, where he composed Rienzi, based on Bulwer Lytton's novel. It is a competent, tuneful work. Wagner and Minna left Riga to escape from their creditors, the sea voyage being rough enough to inspire the stormy seas that surge through *The Flying Dutchman*. They reached Paris in 1840 and endured two bleak years, Wagner being reduced to arranging operas and operettas for cornet solos. However, *Rienzi* was completed, the text of *The Flying Dutchman* was started, and Wagner discovered the legends of *Tannhäuser* and *Lohengrin*.

At last fortune favoured him. He was appointed to the Dresden Court Opera, a production of *Rienzi* having been agreed on. The result in 1842 was a triumph, and in 1843 the *Dutchman* was staged. Even non-Wagnerians can enjoy the opera, yet the authentic voice of the composer is heard, with Wagner's power and virility.

There are echoes of Weber, but the Dutchman's music, the sailors' choruses, Senta's tremendous ballad and other triumphs are signs of growing authority. Redemption through love finishes the opera, a hallmark of Romanticism, which obsessed Wagner perhaps more than any other artist.

Now he turned his study of German medieval legend to operatic use, the result being *Tannhäuser* (1845) based on a 13th-century minstrel of that name and a medieval song contest. Yet we are in a legendary world, the hero tormented with lust for Venus and spiritual passion for Elisabeth. Wagner's fixation with redemption made him twist the legend of Tannhäuser, who returned to the

Eva Randova made a stunning debut at Covent Garden as Ortrud in a new production of Lohengrin *in 1977 by Elijah Moshinsky, conducted by Bernard Haitink. René Kollo sang* Lohengrin, *with Anna Tomowa-Sintow as Elsa, and Donald McIntyre as Telramund.*

Venusburg, and make his hero choose Christian love. The characters are less vivid than those of the Dutchman, but musically the score is full of riches and a notable advance. In 1861 a revised *Tannhäuser* was a failure at the Paris Opéra, with an extended scene on the Venusberg, composed after *Tristan*. The first version of *Tannhäuser* is considered the better artistically.

Back in 1848 Wagner, being in Dresden, had been involved in that Year of Revolutions. Though he had not fought he felt obliged to flee and settled in Zürich, where he and Minna found refuge in a villa on the estate of Otto Wesendonck. He would be an exile until 1861, but his fame increased and he was championed by Franz Liszt. He it was who gave *Lohengrin* its premiere at Weimar in 1850. It was Wagner's last singers' opera – *Die Meistersinger* is a music drama, for all its glorious singing roles – and at last the composer had achieved a total work of art, despite a not very effective first act. Yet the legend of the Swan Knight, combined with the myth of the Holy Grail inspired Wagner to create his first unique artistic world – a *gesamtkunstwerk* – from the very opening of the glorious prelude.

Wagner had now begun what was to be his greatest achievement *Der Ring des Nibelungen* (The Nibelung's Ring, the single Nibelung being Alberich). In fact, he had started work four years earlier with the libretto for *The Death of Siegfried*. From this would come the final *Ring*, which was to be 'a theatre festival play for three days and a preliminary evening'; *Das Rheingold* (The Rhinegold), *Die Walküre* (The Valkyrie), *Siegfried* and *Die Götterdämmerung* (The Twilight of the Gods).

To ease his financial problems he exploited friends and acquaintances alike. He conducted his music for an interested Queen Victoria and had an affair with Frau Wesendonck that helped him compose the ultimate operatic expression of sexual passion, *Tristan und Isolde* (1865). His unfortunate Minna died in 1860, by which time he had begun his lasting relationship with Liszt's daughter Cosima, who was married to the great conductor, Hans von Bülow. Despite his misery, Bülow's championship of Wagner's music did not falter. Then in 1864,

when Wagner appeared to have reached the nadir of his fortunes, he met the ultimate Wagnerite, the lonely, sad King Ludwig of Bavaria. Suddenly, Wagner had no more financial worries.

A production of *Tristan* in Munich in 1865 was the first major result, Ludwig and Malvina Schnorr von Carolsfeld singing the title roles. This was the first of Wagner's mature music dramas and certainly the most intense. Wagner's 'endless melody' had reached perfection, his leitmotivs were miraculously expressive. The symphonic texture is worlds away from earlier operas, though the work can be regarded as the climax of German Romanticism. There are twin themes, longing and renunciation, and the work ends with a *Liebestod* – a love-death –

Viewers were able to experience something of Birgit Nilsson's great Isolde in a profile of the Swedish soprano televised by the BBC in 1972.

unmatched in any sort of drama with the single exception of the last act of Shakespeare's *Antony and Cleopatra*. The opening of *Der Rosenkavalier* is even more sexually explicit, but it pales beside the love scene – feeble words – in Act II of *Tristan*, its music tempestuous, erotic and tender, and with Isolde's confidante Brangäne warning the lovers from offstage in music that adds a layer of matchless beauty to their ecstasy.

Wagner's luck in the world of reality now deserted him. His extravagance and political dabbling made him many enemies at Court, and his hold over the King slipped. He went to Switzerland. Ludwig, however, remained his champion even though Wagner's marriage to Cosima destroyed his close friendship with the

King. Artistically, six years of exile were glorious for he almost finished the *Ring* and completed *Die Meistersinger von Nürnberg*, which was staged in Munich in 1868. In it Wagner created a warmly human, bourgeois world, only the town clerk Beckmesser being (amusingly) unlikable. It was a direct comment on the fine, very influential but anti-Wagnerian critic, Eduard Hanslick, indeed the character began life as Hans Lick. Of course, Wagner was the hero Walter, believer in the new style of music. Yet Wagner, who railed against Jewish influence and anyone who appeared to be in his way, created a work of exceptional charm about ordinary good people, a host of them. As in Shakespeare even tiny roles are three-dimensional, most notably the night watchman who appears for a few glorious moments at the end of Act Two after a riot has subsided. The most famous character (based on a historical one) is the wise, genial cobbler-poet, Hans Sachs. There are set-pieces, the most famous being Walter's Prize Song, and, despite its length, it has always been enormously popular, an inspired blend of characterization, warmth, tunefulness, high spirits, unaffected goodness.

Then came *The Ring. Das Rheingold* was staged in Munich in 1869, *Die Walküre* in 1870, *Siegfried* and *Die Götterdämmerung* at the first Bayreuth Festival in 1876. Without King Ludwig Wagner could not have seen his mighty enterprise through.

The Ring is a total entity though it is in four parts and took more than twenty years to create. A seminal low E flat starts the epic at the bottom of the Rhine. At the end Valhalla is destroyed and the ring of the title is returned to its guardians the Rhinemaidens, as the great river overflows its banks. Redemption through love sounds once again from the orchestra.

Wagner developed his story from the old German Nibelungen sagas, which stem from a German epic poem. He also used the Scandinavian Volsunga Saga. Only specialists know them, but Wagner's transformations of the characters, his flawed gods, his Nibelung dwarfs, his men, women and giants are the ones that have gripped the imaginations of countless thousands.

Each part of the saga has its own flavour, for all the unity of the whole. *Das Rheingold*, the shortest, has the fastest action, with less tension and emotion. It is a perfect introduction to *The Ring* for newcomers, its score, even at first hearing, not being beyond an inexperienced ear. Heroic tragedy follows in *Die Walküre* after a first act that is the most lyrical in the *Ring*. After gods and dwarfs, humanity enters with Siegmund and Sieglinde, and after a scene of the most radiant music the great Sword motif rings out as Siegmund draws the sword from a tree. Even in a short account it must be claimed that Brünnhilde is the most attractive of all Wagner's heroines, while her father Wotan, ruler of the gods, is the most strikingly majestic. This is the most loved of the *Ring* operas, not least because of the

The English National Opera's production of Wagner's The Mastersingers *(Die Meistersinger von Nürnberg), with Norman Bailey as Hans Sachs, Kenneth Woollam as Walther, Kathryn Harries as Eva and Bonaventura Bottone as David.*

Matti Salminen as Fasolt and Fritz Hurner as Fafner alarming Carmen Reppel as Freia in Wagner's Das Rheingold at Bayreuth. The designers of this famous Ring, Richard Peduzzi and Jacques Schmidt, achieved a brilliant melding of myth and modernism. They were, with the producer Patrice Chéreau, abused at first but finally hailed – and their work captured forever on video in 1980.

final scene when Wotan's anger with his daughter vanishes and he leaves her surrounded by magic fire to await a true hero to rouse her from slumber.

Wagner took fifteen years to finish *Siegfried* because of other projects. The work is a blazing shaft of light between two tragedies. The young hero according to Gerhart von Westerman, brings 'thrilling and rhythmic impetus' to the *Ring*. Not until the last act do we leave the marvellous forest idyll and go back to the rock where Brünnhilde lies asleep. A scene of glory is unleashed when she awakens and she and Siegfried greet each other exultantly.

Die Götterdämmerung (The Twilight of the Gods) starts ominously with the Norns foretelling their fall, then we return to Siegfried and Brünnhilde's last moments of happiness. The count-down to catastrophe begins, Wagner providing coup after coup, including his only use of a chorus in the entire *Ring*, for the double wedding ceremony and Siegfried's death. This occurs in a last act of unmatched power, though it starts lightly enough with a scene between Siegfried and the Rhinemaidens. The evil Hagen kills the hero and his Funeral March blazes out

Peter Hofmann as Siegmund and Jeannine Altmeyer as Sieglinde in the famous Patrice Chéreau Ring, conducted by Pierre Boulez.

like the very ending of the world. Yet after Brünnhilde's incomparable last scene and the destruction of the gods' kingdom the glorious melody first heard in the last act of *Die Walküre* surges out. Redemption by love is portrayed in music equalled in *Tristan* but never surpassed.

After *The Ring* came *Parsifal* (1882). This 'stage dedication festival play' was not meant to be performed outside Bayreuth until the copyright expired in 1914, though New York was among those cities that refused to wait. Wagner had intended that this solemn religious work (also steeped in sexuality) should not become part of the general repertoire, though there is a revealing story which contradicts this and shows Wagner as a true man of the theatre. The opera, once usually given without applause, was on one occasion interrupted by vigorous clapping – Wagner himself being the offender.

Parsifal remains the least accessible of Wagner's works, though for some it is the supreme achievement. The hero is the Percival of Malory's *Le Morte D'Arthur*, a

A scene from Die Götterdämmerung, *the last part of the* Ring *cycle. Thanks to video, more people have seen Chéreau's production than all the other* Rings *combined since the first performance of the entire cycle at Bayreuth in August 1876.*

Donald McIntyre as Wotan and Manfred Jung as Siegfried in the Patrice Chéreau Ring.

'simpleton without guile.' A virtual Holy Communion is staged that once created a furore. Some non-Christians found the atmosphere of the work stifling, while Kundry, both Virgin and Venus, upset others. The heart of the story is the Christian legend of the Holy Grail. Leitmotivs are few and the music is harmonically advanced, but clarity itself. Today it is judged solely as a work of art, for the lucky ones a sublime one.

Wagner's colossal influence and the hostility he sparked off is proof of his power. Despite opposition he reached a peak of popularity in the first half of our century, followed by a period when it seemed that he might become a fervent minority interest. Now his operas, helped surely by television, seem to have regained their old mass popularity. In his day he was a leading theatrical figure. At Bayreuth he could lower houselights at a time when everywhere else in Europe auditoriums were lit throughout performances. He would not let in latecomers; he personally raised the standard of

operatic acting, being a fine actor and director himself.

Wagner died in 1883, his wife and son Siegfried continuing to run Bayreuth exactly as it had been, which did no service to his revolutionary genius. Happily, after the Second World War his grandsons, Wieland and Wolfgang, brought about a revolution and made Bayreuth one of the leading theatres, operatic or 'straight', in the world, and so it remains.

Wagner's immediate successors included Hugo Wolf (1860–1903), best known for his *lieder*. His *Der Corregidor* (The Magistrate, 1896), pleasant if undramatic, has lyrical vocal music linked by declamatory passages that show Wagner's influence. Wilhelm Kienzel (1857–1941) started as a Wagnerian, then in his *Der Evangelimann* (The Evangelist, 1895) added Italian *verismo* to his orchestral palette with some success. Yet only Engelbert Humperdinck (1854–1921) wrote a masterpiece that was truly Wagnerian, his children's opera, *Hänsel und Gretel*, complete with

simple nursery tunes. He had assisted Wagner at Bayreuth when *Parsifal* was in rehearsal. Unless badly done his opera cannot fail with children or grown-ups. He could never repeat his triumph, though *Königskinder* (The Royal Children, 1910) was quite successful.

Wagner's son Siegfried (1869–1930) was also a composer, daunting as it must have been for him. He was happy in the land of German fairy-tale opera, his *Der Bärenhäuter* (The Sluggard, 1899) being his best-known work. Composers who reacted against Wagner included the Austro-Hungarian Karl Goldmark (1830–1915) whose *Die Königin von Saba* (The Queen of Sheba 1875) was in the French tradition. Peter Cornelius (1824–74) was influenced by Wagner, but not in his masterpiece, *Der Barbier von Bagdad* (1858), an entertainingly lyrical piece. Hermann Götz (1840–76) was uninfluenced by Wagner in his best opera, *Der Widerspänstigen Zahmung* (1874), inspired by *The Taming of the Shrew*. As is obvious, in Germany at least Wagner had no rivals.

Italy's Age of Glory

BELOW
Rossini's L'Italiana in
Algeri *is one of his most
exhilarating and melodic
scores. English National
Opera's 1979 revival was
a triumph for Elizabeth
Connell as Isabella, for
John Brecknock as
Lindoro, and for the
entire cast.*

'Napoleon is dead' proclaimed the great novelist Stendhal at the start of his biography of Rossini, 'but a new conqueror has already revealed himself to the world; and from Moscow to Naples, from London to Vienna, from Paris to Calcutta, his name is continually on every lip'.

Such splendid overstatement proves that Stendhal was a true opera fanatic, yet he was not exaggerating foolishly in his biography of the great man which ap-

peared in 1824. Rossini's fame was indeed colossal. In Italy at least, he and his great successors, Bellini, Donizetti and, above all, Verdi, achieved a popularity unique in the history of the performing arts. Only the drama of Elizabethan and Jacobean England has arguably gripped people of all classes to such a degree.

But opera's hold lasted far longer, certainly to the death of Puccini in 1924. It was a hold as strong as a national sport,

and combined with patriotism, with the feelings of millions of Italians longing for nationhood. And at the centre was a man able to give those feelings musical life, Giuseppe Verdi.

Gioacchino Rossini was born in Pesaro in 1792, the son of a trumpeter and a singer, the infant timing his entrance for February 29. He studied at Bologna and his first opera, *Demetrio e Polibio*, written at the Conservatory, would later be staged in 1812. Several operas followed before he had his first great success with *La Pietra del Paragone* (The Touchstone, 1812). It was given at La Scala and for the first time an audience heard the soon to be famous Rossini crescendo. An amazing six months followed which saw four premieres in Venice, including *L'Italiana in Algeri* (The Italian Girl in Algiers) with as tuneful a score as he ever wrote, and *Tancredi*, that made him famous beyond Italy. The opera has some of Rossini's

most tender love music. It is a serious piece, a heroic melodrama.

Rossini cannot be claimed as a musical revolutionary; he just happened to be better at writing operas than any Italian since Monteverdi. His melodies, orchestration, exhilarating crescendos and intoxicating high spirits led to genuine Rossini fever raging in Europe. Some of his more ornamental arias may seem facile today, too ornamented and less pleasing than Donizetti's, yet when properly sung doubts usually crumble. *Il Turco in Italia* (1814), though entertaining, was (rightly) considered not as good as *The Italian Girl in Algiers* while *Sigismondo* failed.

Rossini was now engaged by Domenico Barbaia, an ex-waiter turned circus owner, turned impresario, who was running Naples' two opera houses, the Teatro San Carlo (still a national glory) and the Teatro del Fondo. Barbaia's mistress was the reigning prima donna, Isabella Colbran, who would later be Rossini's mistress and wife. She sang the lead in *Elisabetta, Regina d'Inghilterra* (1815), an entertaining piece whose recitatives had a string accompaniment, and whose ornaments were fully written out and not left to the singer's imagination or lack of it.

Torvaldo e Dorliska (1815) was a failure in Rome, and Naples saw the premiere of *Il Barbiere di Siviglia* in 1816. Paisiello,

ABOVE
Frederica von Stade and David Rendall in La Donna del Lago *by Donizetti after Scott's novel. It was produced at Covent Garden in 1985 using sets seen earlier at Houston. Marilyn Horne sang the role of Malcolm.*

revered in Naples, had composed a successful *Barbiere* (1782) himself and Rossini's met a hostile audience on the night of 20 February. But the second night was a triumph, and later in the same year he enjoyed another success with *Otello*, which remained popular until Verdi's opera killed it. Rossini gave his opera a happy ending after the true one upset the Neapolitans.

His output was prodigious. 1817 alone saw *La Cenerentola* (Cinderella), *La Gazza Ladra* (The Thieving Magpie), *Armida* and *Adelaide di Borgogna*, the only failure. In 1818 came *Mosè in Egitto* (later *Moïse* in Paris), which always startles those who know nothing of the powerful, serious Rossini, the predecessor of Verdi. In the ten years since *Tancredi* Rossini had composed twenty-five operas, many revived in modern times after being neglected, like *Semiramide* (1823), forgotten except for its overture until Joan Sutherland and Richard Bonynge revived the monumental work in the 1960s.

In Vienna Beethoven urged Rossini to give the world more *Barbers*; in England he sang duets with George IV. He settled in Paris, where in 1828 he surpassed himself with a sparkling sophisticated comedy, *Le Comte Ory* (1828). It contains a trio worthy of his beloved Mozart. The libretto is a French one, but Rossini's spell in charge of the Théatre Italien served Italian opera well. He lived on until 1868, but his operatic career ended in 1829 with his magnificent *Guillaume Tell*, the millions who only know its overture having little idea of its greatness and melodic glory.

The 1830 Revolution put paid to four contracted operas so Rossini became a Parisian institution, a gourmet, and an occasional writer of tuneful religious music. He never lost his interest in music, hailing Verdi 'at last' after hearing *Rigoletto* and brilliantly calling Offenbach 'the Mozart of the Champs-Elysées'. He did not explain his extended 'rest' from opera, but he deserved his leisure. He was buried in Paris, but Italy reclaimed his body in 1887, where huge crowds greeted the coffin. A choir of 300 sang his great Prayer from his *Moses* – so well that an encore was demanded.

Vincenzo Bellini (1801–35) was Rossini's first major successor, a Sicilian and a

Romantic. The composer of some of the longest melodies in opera, he was a marvellous, sometimes sublime, writer of tunes. British critics and musicians, steeped in the German tradition, were dismissive of him earlier in our century; his masterpiece *Norma* apart, indeed he was little known outside Italy. Times changed and Callas appeared, and now, as long as there are the singers, Bellini will never again vanish from the repertoire.

These singers have to sustain Bellini's mighty lines. He once expressed the wish that he could write opera at which his

listeners would die with singing. *Norma* has a libretto by a master, Felici Romani which inspired Bellini to excel himself. He was a master of dramatic recitative, as Callas, above all, demonstrated in the 1950s. Born in Catania, his first opera, *Adelson e Salvina* (1825) demonstrated his lyric gift to the Neapolitans. *Bianca e Fernando* followed, then came real success at La Scala with *Il Pirata* in 1827. The title role was created for the great Giovanni Battista Rubini, while the music with its long, languorous melodies was a break from the florid style of Rossini. *La*

Straniera (The Stranger) and *Zaira* followed, then the very beautiful Romeo and Juliet opera, *I Capuleti e i Montecchi*, first given in Venice in 1830.

The next year was Bellini's finest for it was the year of *La Sonnambula* (The Sleepwalker) and *Norma*. Set in Switzerland, *La Sonnambula* is an idyll about the sleepwalker Amina. It has ravishing melodies and the libretto was praised by the demanding Wagner for the way that music and words blended.

The first Amina was Giudetta Pasta, a great actress-singer, who would also

Rossini's La Cenerentola *(Cinderella) at La Scala, Milan, with Frederica von Stade in the title role. Claudio Abbado was the conductor and Jean-Pierre Ponelle the producer. The opera's premiere was in Rome in 1817.*

RIGHT
A scene from Rossini's The Barber of Seville (Il Barbiere di Siviglia) *staged by Welsh National Opera in 1986. The opera is performed in a town square on a travelling stage, the singers having a very busy evening. Della Jones was Rosina, Gwion Thomas, Figaro, Peter Bronder, the Count, Donald Adams, Bartolo and William Mackie, Basilio.*

OPPOSITE TOP
Suzanne Murphy in the great title role of Bellini's Norma, *staged by Welsh National Opera in 1985. As well as the excellent protagonist, Kathryn Harries was very fine as Adalgisa, with good support from Frederick Donaldson and Harry Dworchak.*

OPPOSITE BOTTOM
Henriette Sontag (1806–54) was a German soprano particularly famous in Mozart, Bellini and Donizetti. She is seen here in the title role of Bellini's La Sonnambula (The Sleepwalker).

create Norma and Donizetti's Anna Bolena, partnered by another legendary artist, the tenor Rubini. Bellini later heard Maria Malibran, García's daughter, in the role at Drury Lane in London, and went nearly mad with delight at the most thrilling actress-singer of the day. She died aged twenty-eight, mourned by artists, writers and poets as well as musicians.

Norma was first performed at La Scala in 1831 with Pasta as the heroine, one of the most taxing roles in opera, also one of the grandest and noblest. Its opening aria, 'Casta diva' (Chaste goddess) would have proved Bellini a master if he had written nothing else. The opera is simply scored – for Bellini was particularly concerned with the voice – simply but effectively. It concerns Norma, a Druid high-priestess who has dared to love a Roman. The libretto by Romani is a fine one, the opera, with the right singers – Callas especially in modern times – is magnificent.

Beatrice di Tenda (1833) was not so successful, though it anticipates Verdi, but *I Puritani* (1835), without Romani, set in England but about the Puritans of Scotland, is melodically unmatched, like its mad scene. This darling of the Romantics died tragically young.

The line of glory continued with Gaetano Donizetti (1797–1848), composer of some seventy-five operas. Many have been performed since the revival of interest in the age of *bel canto*, a few of them masterpieces, virtually all, it would seem, worth hearing. By the 1940s he was little known outside Italy except at the Metropolitan, in Britain only *Don Pasquale* (1843) being staged occasionally. Now the combination of Callas and changing tastes have ensured that a number of his operas are heard regularly. His first major work, *Anna Bolena* (1830) had Pasta and Rubini in the La Scala cast. Callas made the role her own there in Visconti's 1957 production. Other operas, now known or well known, include the delectable comedy, *L'Elisir d'Amore*, *Lucrezia Borgia*, *Maria Stuarda*, *La Fille du Régiment* with a French text, the fine grand opera, *La Favorite*, and the masterpiece, *Lucia di Lammermoor*, premiered at the height of the Romantic Age in 1835. Callas and Sutherland – the latter over many years – have excelled in the role in modern times.

A scene from John Copley's delightful production of Donizetti's L'Elisir d'Amore *at Covent Garden in 1975, conducted by John Pritchard. Centre stage is Sir Geraint Evans as the quack doctor Dulcamara, one of the great Welsh baritone's celebrated characterizations.*

Donizetti wrote too much too fast to maintain a regularly high standard. He wrote for singers in an age of great singing. Jauntiness is liable to break in at serious moments, but he attained occasional greatness and is widely loved, except by the austere. Alas, his contemporary Saverio Mercadante wrote some sixty operas, but is very rarely performed. Yet he provided richer orchestration and more dramatic force than most of his rivals. The greatest of all Italian opera composers admired him, and it is to Giuseppe Verdi (1813–1901) that we now turn.

Verdi's great career was Shakespearean. His comparatively crude early operas already had a dynamic vitality that his contemporaries rarely matched, and in old age it was Shakespeare who inspired him to a place in opera's Valhalla inhabited only by Mozart and Wagner.

Little over a generation ago in Britain it would have been impossible to write such an opening paragraph about Verdi without seeming controversial. Francis Toye's brilliant biography in 1931 was a defensive one. A poet had written: 'The music's only Verdi but the melody is sweet.' Today, the only danger is too many superlatives. In the 1950s Ernest Newman roasted *La Forza del Destino* for not being built on Wagnerian lines!

In Italy Verdi's star has never waned, though his earlier works had dropped out of the standard repertoire. For many outside Italy Verdi meant *Rigoletto, La Traviata, Il Trovatore* and *Aida*. The *Requiem* was considered too operatic. Germany began the Verdi revival in the 1920s, and by the 1950s and '60s it was possible for a Londoner to enjoy virtually the entire canon, *Un Giorno di Regno*, his

second opera, included. It had been previously written off as a total failure.

Verdi was born at La Roncole near Busseto in the Duchy of Parma. A plaque there calls him 'the pure expression of the soul of the Italian people.' For all the universal love he inspires today, he can never mean so much, even to his own people, as he did when he was the musical expression of an Italy longing to be free of the Austrian yoke. In 1814 the Austrians were at war with their great enemy to the East, and a detachment of Russian soldiers looted Verdi's village, killing women and children while the baby and his mother hid in a belfry. The local organist was his first teacher, and Antonio Barezzi, a music lover whose daughter he was to marry, helped him. Failing to get in to the Conservatory at Milan, he became an organist and conductor of the band of his home town, Busseto. *Rochester*, his first opera, is lost, but *Oberto, Conte di San Bonifacio*, was staged at La Scala in 1839, partly because the soprano, Giuseppina Strepponi, was interested in it, and, indeed, in its creator. She became his mistress then his wife. Verdi had lost his first wife and their two children in a short space of time. The Scala's manager Merelli offered Verdi a contract for three more operas, but he was deeply depressed. Artistically the tragedies would add dimensions of feelings to his father-

Andrei Serban's production of Bellini's I Puritani, *revived by Welsh National Opera in 1986, is remarkably realistic, more so than the libretto. On the left are Suzanne Murphy and Dennis O'Neill as the lovers, Elvira and Arturo.*

daughter scenes in *Rigoletto* and *Simon Boccanegra*, but now the outlook was bleak, bleaker still when his second opera, *Un Giorno di Regno* (King for a Day) failed totally in 1840. Yet like in *Oberto* the seeds of future glories were there.

Merelli still believed in the young man and offered him the libretto of *Nabuco-donosor*, soon to be known as *Nabucco*. It fell open at the point where the Jewish exiles by the waters of Babylon long for their homeland. This historic moment led to a return to composing and the hauntingly magnificent chorus, 'Va

pensiero, sull ali dorate', which would become a national anthem in the fight for Italian independence, and which still has a place in Italian hearts for patriotic as well as musical reasons.

Nabucco and its successors appeal directly to the emotions, but unlike some of those that followed, it is a masterpiece. The sophisticated might sigh but opera-goers rejoiced in the great swinging tunes, the warmth and vitality, the new voice committed totally to the characters. That it was harmonically and rhythmically unpretentious mattered not at all. The

first Abigaille, the heroine, was Strepponi, who left the theatre seven years later; she went to live with Verdi and married him in 1859.

I Lombardi alli Prima Crociata (The Lombards at the First Crusade) scored a success in 1843 and the finer *Ernani* the next year had a libretto by Francesco Maria Piave after Victor Hugo's *Hernani*. The vengeful Silva in *Ernani* is a magnificent creation. These years were called his 'galley years' by Verdi, but his success was colossal. The sophisticated might prefer Bellini and Donizetti – Robert Browning was one such – but the public took Verdi to their hearts: Donizetti, on hearing *I Due Foscari*, announced: 'Frankly, this man is a genius.' He saw through the somewhat primitive strength and blazing melodramatics to the crux of the matter – that Verdi was a born opera composer. *Giovanna d'Arco* and *Alzira* followed in 1845 and *Attila* the next year, complete with fiery *cabalettas* and passionate melodies. *Attila* opened in Venice in 1846, the Venetians being able to enjoy the birth of their city on stage in a scene of simple powerful grandeur. The librettist

Alfredo Kraus and Joan Sutherland at Covent Garden in 1980 in Donizetti's Lucrezia Borgia, *conducted by Richard Bonynge. Not ideal as a villainess, Sutherland sang superbly, while Alfredo Kraus astonished even his many admirers by his splendidly stylish singing.*

Solera contributed a line that became a battle cry: 'Avrai ti l'universo, Resti l'Italia a me' – 'You may have the universe, let Italy remain mine!'

Verdi's first music drama – not a phrase he used – was *Macbeth* (1847, revised 1865). The sleepwalking scene apart, it would be wrong to claim that it rivals Shakespeare, but it is a fine work with well-drawn characters, only an excess of witches being questionable. The sound of a town band as Duncan arrives at the castle had been abused, yet it is a brilliant touch, the jolly music contrasting with the tragedy to come. Lady Macbeth is the opera's dominant figure – Verdi's thinking had gone beyond *bel canto* now. He wanted Lady Macbeth's voice to be 'hard, stifled and dark . . . the voice of a devil'. He wanted vocal acting not simply beautiful tone and believable acting from his singers. In his eighties he leapt on stage to demonstrate to Francesco Tamagno, his stiff Otello, what he wanted. Verdi could not insist of acting standards to rival Bayreuth's with its festival conditions. In his day those who could act did so, the rest, unless urged, did not. It can still happen today.

I *Masnadieri* (The Brigands, 1847) had its premiere in London with Jenny Lind, the Swedish Nightingale, in the lead, Verdi conducting, and the Queen, Prince Albert and the opera-loving Duke of Wellington in the audience. It was cheered – rightly – but *Il Corsaro* the following year is probably Verdi's least inspired score. *La Battaglia di Legnano* (1849) was much better, indeed the whole fourth act was encored, and we are told that a soldier present was so enflamed that he flung his accoutrements on the stage, then jumped out of his box. Revolutionary flames were fanned, a very rare event in the history of art.

The delightful *Luisa Miller* followed in 1849, a warm, intimate work, then came the last opera of the galley years, *Stiffelio*, rewritten as *Aroldo* (1850/57) a minor piece with – as always – fine moments. Three masterpieces followed, *Rigoletto*, *Il Trovatore* and *La Traviata*, the first in 1851, the others in 1853. *Rigoletto* was Verdi's first work of complete genius. Piave adapted *Le Roi S'Amuse* by Victor Hugo, changing the king into the Duke of Mantua for censorship reasons, reigning

LEFT
Luciano Pavarotti as Radames in Aida *at Covent Garden in 1984. It was produced and designed by Jean-Pierre Ponelle and conducted by Zubin Mehta. The Russian bass, Paata Burchuladze, in the supporting role of Ramfis, the High Priest, made a striking impression.*

As millions have heard and seen on TV direct from Verona, Franco Bonisolli and the remarkable veteran mezzo, Fiorenza Cossotto, were in great form in Verona's huge arena in Il Trovatore *in 1985. Cossotto made her debut in 1957.*

monarchs not being permitted to be seen as libertines in the Italian theatre. Also, since the revolutions of 1848, an attempt to kill a sovereign on stage in the final act was anathema to the Austrian rulers of Venice, where the great work had its premiere. Verdi triumphed mightily.

With its melodic riches and fine dramatic structure, with the character of the flawed hunchback hero, the opera was bound to succeed. The greatest moment in the title role is Rigoletto's feigned gaiety while seeking his abducted daughter, as he pleads with the courtiers and finally rounds on them. The leading parts are all well characterized, while the great quartet in the last act – in fact, it is a double duet – was one of the two moments that reconciled Hugo to the opera,

the other being the sombre scene between Rigoletto and Sparafucile, the hired assassin.

Il Trovatore (The Troubador, 1853) is dramatically less convincing, but full of thrilling and beautiful tunes. Contrary to legend, the libretto is adequate because the situations are strong and the characters at least two dimensional. The Miserere and the Anvil Chorus are known far beyond the opera house, while Leonora's 'D'Amor sull'ali rosee' is worthy of Bellini at his best.

La Traviata (The Woman Gone Astray, 1853) is based on Dumas the Younger's *La Dame aux Camélias*, a good enough play turned by Verdi into a strong and tender masterpiece. Toscanini praised its 'truthfulness', one of a number of reasons for its enduring popularity. The consumptive heroine Violetta, based on a real character, has most glorious and varied music, challenging because she ranges from coloratura to passionate drama. Like Carmen, the role suffers badly when the heroine is physically miscast, as was the first one, Fanny Salvini-Donatelli. The tenor was out of voice, and the baritone resented the size of his part! It used to be said that the first performance failed also because it was given in the clothes of the day, but Harold Rosenthal has found that this did not occur. It is an intimate music-drama of surpassing charm and feeling, words that describe Teresa Stratas' performance in the Zeffirelli film.

Les Vêpres Siciliennes (The Sicilian Vespers, 1853) was written for La Grande Boutique (The great toyshop), as Verdi described the Paris Opéra. It is the only one of Verdi's later works to be somewhat neglected. Its fine score is not as memorable as most later Verdi operas and the composer was unsatisfied with the French text. *Simon Boccanegra* (1857, revised 1881) is a far finer work, set in Genoa, often sombre in mood but with magnificent scenes that have made it very popular. We usually hear a combination of the two versions. As in a number of Verdi operas there is a deeply emotional scene between a father and a daughter.

Verdi became a politician, albeit a token one. After years of strife and disappointments Italian unity had been achieved and he was asked by Cavour to serve in the new Italian parliament. He served quietly from 1861–65, Cavour being aware of Verdi's symbolic value to his country. So many of his early operas had a core of patriotic fervour, but Verdi meant even more to the Risorgimento. His very name had been a concealed rallying cry, for VIVA VERDI written on walls meant *Viva Vittorio Emanuele, Re D'Italia*.

Just before his time in parliament Verdi's *Un Ballo in Maschera* (A Masked Ball, 1859) was written. It blends tragedy and comedy, lightness, drama and humour, but the censors objected that the assassination of a king, Gustavus III of Sweden, was shown on stage. The action was therefore transferred to Boston in the 17th century, hard for an Anglo-Saxon

A memorable production of Nabucco, Verdi's first great success, opened the season at La Scala, Milan in December 1986. Baritone Renato Bruson sang the title role, with Ghena Dimitrova as Abigaille and Paata Burchuladze as Zaccaria, High Priest of Jerusalem. Riccardo Muti conducted: the occasion also marked his return to La Scala as Music Director.

The 1985 production at the Arena di Verona of Attila. From left to right: Mario Ferrara, Maria Chiara, Yevgeny Nesterenko in the title role, and Silvano Carroli.

One of the most famous scenes in the history of opera in Britain, the last act of Jonathan Miller's 'Mafia' Rigoletto, a jewel in English National Opera's crown. First staged in 1982, this is the 1985 revival. John Rawnsley and Valerie Masterson were Rigoletto and Gilda, Arthur Davies, 'Duke', and Jean Rigby, Maddalena.

Luisa Miller is one of the finest of Verdi's early works and melodically very rich. Seen here are Pavarotti and Ricciarelli at Covent Garden in 1978 as Rodolfo and Luisa.

RIGHT
Two artists who have shot to fame during the 1980s, Rosalind Plowright as Leonora and Giorgio Zancanaro as the Count in Verdi's Il Trovatore at the Arena di Verona in 1985.

audience to respond to. Yet the melodies are superb and the principals well characterized, making it one of Verdi's most popular works. *La Forza del Destino* followed in 1862, a sprawling masterpiece, complete with coincidences, but with a score that allays criticisms of its stageworthiness. It was first staged in St. Petersburg, where it annoyed nationalist composers who wanted recognition.

Verdi now revised *Macbeth*, then wrote *Don Carlos*, a Parisian grand opera that is now adored, as it has been in Britain since the Giulini-Visconti production of the work at Covent Garden in 1958. Purists reasonably complain that it should be given in French. Based on Schiller's play, it presents a teeming and believable world. It is subtle, passionate, even epic and very human, its Act IV Scene I being often claimed as the greatest scene in all Italian opera. This begins with King Philip of Spain's deeply-felt 'Ella giammai m'amo' (She has no love for me) about his wife, continues with a vivid scene between the King and the Grand Inquisitor (another bass), then, after other glories, it ends with 'O don fatale (O fatal gift) sung by Eboli, the King's mistress. Carlos's friend Rodrigo, having shared a famous duet earlier in the opera, has a tremendous and touching death scene, while the Queen's final aria, 'Tu che le vanitá', has a line of melody like a great arch. This is surely Verdi's noblest score.

Aida followed in 1871, eternally popular, unsinkable even with poor staging as long as the singers are right, and with characters so well drawn that they are not dwarfed by the opera's scenes of pageantry. Musically the finest scenes are in Act III beside the Nile and Amneris's passionate outburst in the penultimate scene. The opera is the ideal one for the Verona Arena in front of 25,000 people, yet *Aida* has glorious intimate scenes.

Verdi revised *Boccanegra* in 1881, helped by his finest librettist, the composer Arrigo Boito (1842–1918). The younger man had been influenced by Beethoven and Wagner and had even attacked Verdi in print. He might write about the honour of Italian music being 'befouled by the filth of the brothel' but wrote sensitively about 'Quando le sere al placido' in Verdi's *Luisa Miller*. Boito's own *Mefistofele* (1868) was not a success at

La Scala, but it is an impressive work based on the first part of Goethe's *Faust*. The pair became closer and it was Boito who wrote the incomparable librettos for *Otello* (1887) and *Falstaff* (1894).

The former is the perfect tragic opera. Boito's compression of Shakespeare is brilliant, beginning with the landing at Cyprus and providing Verdi with the springboard for the most exciting opening in opera. Verdi's Desdemona is stronger than Shakespeare's and her Willow Song is simple and sublime. Only a true heroic tenor can do justice to Otello's music, which begins with a great outburst, *Esultate!* When Iago enflames the jealous Otello in Act II Verdi matches Shakespeare. Even the drinking song in Act I is an expression of character with danger lurking beneath it, while Iago's evil nature is magnificently realized. This is Verdi's supreme opera.

Audiences have never warmed quite as much to Verdi's last opera, *Falstaff*, based very closely on Shakespeare's *The Merry Wives of Windsor*, but with clever interpolations of parts of *Henry IV*, notably the 'Honour' monologue. The score is scintillatingly fast, while two moments are particularly vivid. One is the jealous Ford's impassioned outburst when Verdi, like a true Shakespearean, injects seriousness into a farcical situation. The other is when Falstaff, the born survivor, has a paean of self-esteem, 'Va, vecchio John,' summing up the essence of the born survivor, a superb affirmation of the life-force and

June Anderson as Violetta in Welsh National Opera's La Traviata in 1984. In 1987 this brilliant American soprano enjoyed another success at Covent Garden in Lucia di Lammermoor.

Man, the unconquerable optimist. At the very end of the opera, the composer who failed·to get into the Milan Conservatory, finished it with a choral fugue of volcanic high spirits.

Verdi was a complicated man, less likable than sentimentalists allow. He was affected by his struggles. He was a flawed hero, but a hero indeed, rightly loved as well as revered. No operatic composer is more virile and melodious than he. More than 200,000 lined the streets of Milan to bid him farewell, and they sang the great chorus from *Nabucco* as they did years later when his greatest interpreter, Arturo Toscanini, died. The poet D'Annunzio wrote of Verdi: '*Pianse e amo per tutti*' – 'He wept and loved for all.' Francis Toye, a biographer of Verdi stated that the

Ileana Cotrubas and Luis
Lima, both ideally cast as
Elizabeth de Valois and
Carlos in a revival of
Verdi's Don Carlos at
Covent Garden in 1985.

The notable American
baritone, Sherrill Milnes,
sang the title role in
Verdi's Simon
Boccanegra at Covent
Garden in 1980, with
Kiri Te Kanawa as the
Doge's daughter Amelia,
Robert Lloyd (right) as
Jacopo Fiesco and
Veriano Luchetti as
Gabriele Adorno.

literal translation gives little idea of the implication of the Italian, but he was writing before the Verdi revival was truly under way. Now when Verdi's star can never set as long as opera lasts, countless operagoers understand what the poet so movingly expressed.

The lesser composers of a golden age, even those with considerable talent, can be cruelly neglected, more so today when costs spell risk. Petrella, Pisani, Pedrotti, Montuoro, Platania and Marchetti are names only known to specialists today, yet Verdi's constant companion after his Giuseppina's death, the magnificent Bohemian soprano Teresa Stolz, sang in operas by them between 1865 and 1871.

The other Italian operas remembered between *Don Pasquale* in 1843 and Mascagni's *Cavalleria Rusticana* in 1890, apart from *Mefistofele*, already discussed, only number two, *La Gioconda* and *La Wally*. Mascagni's influential works be-

Grace Bumbry, the distinguished American mezzo, in one of her most famous roles, Amneris in Aida. She made her debut in the role at the Paris Opéra in 1960.

long later, but the other two are very much part of their period.

La Gioconda (The Joyful Girl, 1876) by Amilcare Ponchielli is the only one of his nine operas to survive in the repertoire, deservedly because it is a superb vehicle for singers. The Metropolitan, New York, with its stellar casts, has let the old warhorse loose regularly down the years. In forty years of operagoing the present author has seen it on television and once attended a concert performance.

La Wally by Alfredo Catalani (1854–93) was loved by Toscanini, who named his daughter after the heroine. His *Loreley* is also heard in Italy and sometimes beyond. German romanticism influenced the composer, whose finest music has a noble quality. La Wally's one already famous aria, 'Ebben, n'andro lontana', shot to international popularity through the film *Diva*. The opera's lovers perish in an avalanche.

It is unlikely that some unknown treasure from the age of Verdi will emerge. The finest pages of Boito's *Mefistofele* are in the same league as Verdi's, and one aria, 'L'altra notte', in which Marguerite hauntingly describes the drowning of her baby, is one of the most overwhelming moments in Italian opera.

RIGHT
The Russian mezzo, Elena Obraztsova, as Santuzza in Zeffirelli's film of Cavalleria Rusticana. *Domingo sang Turridu and Renato Bruson, Alfio.*

PRECEDING PAGE TOP
The Royal Opera House staged a new production of Verdi's Falstaff *in 1982, conducted by Carlo Maria Giulini and produced by Ronald Eyre. Renato Bruson sang the title role, with Katia Ricciarelli as Alice, Lucia Valentini-Terrani as Mistress Quickly and Leo Nucci as Ford. This production, first seen in Los Angeles in 1982, was too sober for some tastes, albeit brilliantly conducted.*

PRECEDING PAGE BOTTOM
That overworked word fabulous is the only way to describe the career of Luigi Lablache. This great Italian bass sang in Mozart's Requiem *at Beethoven's funeral, gave Queen Victoria singing lessons, was the first Riccardo in Bellini's* I Puritani, *and was the first Don Pasquale. The drawing is a reminder that operatic music was the pop music of his day – 1794–1858.*

French Gravity and Gaiety

The French school of opera tends to be underrated outside France, yet Paris has been an operatic centre since the 17th century, not least because so many foreign composers and musicians settled there. That said, the two geniuses of 19th-century French opera, Hector Berlioz and Georges Bizet, had careers so frustrating and often wretched that it is easy to become biased against the Parisian establishment. It does not help that too little French opera is heard outside France, while during our century the reputation of French singing has decreased. Happily, the Paris Opéra re-established itself in the 1970s as a major international force. At the exact time of writing the Opéra is presenting a star-studded *Elektra* with Hildegard Behrens and Christa Ludwig, conducted by Seiji Ozawa, while at the Salle Favart Lully's *Atys* is being given, first staged in 1676.

When Gluck died in 1787 he left no clear successor. Etienne-Nicolas Méhul

(1763–1817), Napoleon's favourite composer, is remembered today for his overtures, but his *Joseph* (1807) was liked in France and Germany for many years, despite an all male cast. Luigi Cherubini (1760–1842) settled in France and was the very influential and conservative Director of the Conservatoire from 1821 until he died. His masterpiece, *Médée*, gave Callas another of her legendary roles. *Lodoiska* (1791) and *Les Deux Journées* (The Two Days, 1800), also known as *The Water Carrier* were both successes. The latter is a Romantic opera, the hero escaping from 17th-century Paris in a barrel.

Also from Italy was Gasparo Spontini (1774–1851), whose most famous work is *La Vestale* (yet another Callas revival in the 1950s). Produced in 1807, it made his name, while he also raised standards at the Opéra. Wagner's *Rienzi* shows Spontini's influence. Napoleon decided that Spontini's *Fernand Cortez* (1809) might be useful propaganda for his Spanish war. Spontini himself preferred his *Olympie* (1819).

The very critical Berlioz admired Spontini because he raised operatic standards and was a forerunner of French grand opera, but the Romantic Movement made him seem outdated after the triumph of *Der Freischütz*, by which time he was head of the Berlin Court Opera. A notable link between two ages, he died in Italy.

Rossini's move to Paris has been noted, and his influence on French grand opera. This had continuous music and, usually, historic and heroic plots, *opéra comique* having dialogue in place of recitatives, but not necessarily being comic. Ordinary people feature in the genre, heroes being in grand opera at the Opéra, where never a word was spoken on stage.

Daniel Auber (1782–1871) is best remembered today for his racy overtures, yet *Fra Diavolo* (1830) is a tuneful and entertaining piece. Auber wrote many operas with Eugène Scribe, a much-used librettist who, with Germain Delavigne, helped make history. Some playwrights like to believe that they can influence events, but few have, though they can help change the climate of opinion, as John Osborne did in *Look Back in Anger*. Their champions claim even more. Yet Auber and his librettists helped start a revolution. The opera was *La Muette de Portici* (1828), better known as *Masaniello*, the place Brussels in 1830, and its effect was even greater than *La Battaglia di Legnano*'s premiere. Based on a Neapolitan uprising against the Spaniards in 1647, when it was staged in Brussels in 1830 it triggered off the Belgian Revolution against the Dutch. It was 25 August 1830, and the audience, carried away by the heroic story, ran into the streets when it was over and started a train of events that led to independence.

Three other French composers of that time are not forgotten, Adrien Boïeldieu (1775–1834), composer of *La Dame Blanche* (1825) a superb *opéra comique*; Fromental Halevy (1799–1862), a French Jew whose finest opera is *La Juive* (1835); and Ferdinand Hérold (1791–1833), whose *Zampa* is best known today for its overture. Meanwhile the composer Giacomo Meyerbeer (1791–1864) is better known than any of them but still awaits true rediscovery. Rich, envied and,

Atys by Lully dates from 1676. The composer founded French opera and was also very influential in the development of ballet. Lully was born in Italy, came to Paris as a boy and was finally made operatic director by Louis XIV.

indeed, hated, this German Jew was the supreme exponent of French grand opera. Abused by those who know little of him, in his day stars longed to be in his works, operas that were impressive if not great ones. He helped Wagner (who abused him in print) by persuading Berlin to stage *Rienzi* and *The Flying Dutchman* there. That he softened up critics with presents is not a hanging offence.

Starting his career in Venice, he went to Paris and, helped by Scribe, was a one man Common Market, using German methods, Italianate melodies and his new French sense of identity. He also started thinking big, surpassing past efforts to achieve grandeur – huge crowd scenes, vast ensembles and a notable and much acclaimed 'resurrection of the nuns', a ballet that starred the ghosts of nuns who had discovered sex before they died in *Robert le Diable* (1831).

Bigger still was *Les Huguenots* (1836) complete with the Massacre of St. Bartholomew. If it can be afforded, this is a marvellous work and was much praised by Wagner's enemy Hanslick; indeed Wagner himself praised parts of it. It requires six stars, seven if possible. At New York's Metropolitan Opera on 26 December 1894 it got them: Melba, Jean and Edouard de Reszke, Nordica, Plançon, Maurel and Sofia Scalchi, a stellar cluster who provided the fabulous *les nuits de sept étoiles*.

Meyerbeer became the King of Prussia's musical director in 1842. His later works included *L'Étoile du Nord*, *Dinorah* – both French *opéras comiques* – and,

posthumously performed, his masterpiece, *L'Africaine* about the explorer Vasco da Gama. It was more than six hours long at first, and contains the radiant aria best known by its Italian title, *O Paradiso*.

Hector Berlioz's career was far less fortunate. Born in 1803 (he died in 1869) he was either his nation's greatest operatic genius or a flawed master. His operatic career began in the 1830s, the age of Auber and Meyerbeer, an age of enter-

tainments like Adolphe Adam's delightful *Le Postillon de Longjumeau* (1836). Into this world came a non-conformist who, except outside the opera house, could not get himself accepted.

His first opera, *Benvenuto Cellini* (1838), was the only one staged in his lifetime. It is a youthful, high-spirited work centred round the casting of the historical Cellini's statue of Perseus for the Pope, a highspot being the Roman Carnival scene. Comedy, seriousness and the her-

oic are not blended ideally, but the characters are adequate and the music superb. It had many admirers at the Opéra, but the controversial young composer was much criticized. Then the great tenor Duprez left the cast and it was taken off. Liszt presented it at Weimar in 1852 and Covent Garden the next year, but there it was driven off the stage, so Berlioz wrote, by 'a gang of Italians' hissing, booing and shouting. For years only its overture and additional overture, the sparkling *Le*

Carnival Romain, were known. Berlioz died in 1869.

Le Damnation de Faust (1846) was not staged until 1893 at Monte Carlo, Jean de Reszke singing Faust, yet the work, if imaginatively produced, is superb. But it was not written as an opera. Poor Berlioz, one of the greatest dramatic composers, had to abandon the art form that suited him best. The French were happier with talent than genius. It came about therefore that *Les Troyens* (1856–58), for many his masterpiece, was not given in full (over two nights) until 1890 at Karlsruhe, though a mutilated version of Part 2 was given at the Théâtre-Lyrique in Paris in 1863. The two parts are *La Prise de Troie* (The Capture of Troy) and *Les Troyens à Carthage*.

Les Troyens makes a long evening, but so do many of Wagner's operas. The present author considers it a total masterpiece. It has been occasionally staged in cut versions in France. Since Covent Garden's almost complete version in 1957, with Kubelik as conductor and Gielgud as producer, the work being given over one legendary evening with Jon Vickers an incomparable Aeneas, the opera has become reasonably well known, not least because of a definitive recording under Sir Colin Davis. Boston, New York, Glasgow

Benvenuto Cellini by Berlioz was revived at Covent Garden in 1966 with Nicolai Gedda outstanding in the title role. David Ward was the Pope and Elizabeth Vaughan was Teresa. John Dexter produced, making the most of the famous Roman Carnival scene, as did the conductor, John Pritchard.

(in the '30s and '60s), Florence and San Francisco have staged the work, not always completely, the first complete French version being at Covent Garden in 1968.

Berlioz fashioned his own libretto. He thought big and could fashion dramatic effects even without music, while his characterization is excellent, even in tiny parts. Hylas, a young sailor, has a song in which he yearns for home in which the Mediterranean steals through the accompaniment, while in Part I Andromache, Hector's widow, has a mute entrance to music which rivals Gluck's 'Dance of the

There was a time when Gounod's *Faust* was the most popular opera in the repertoire, and it still draws large audiences. Out of fashion in sophisticated circles, the very success of *Faust* made him think himself a master of the grand manner, and grandeur sometimes turned to the grandiose, even the religiose. In Germany, the opera is called *Margarethe*, under which name it can be enjoyed without thought of Goethe's masterpiece.

Charles Gounod (1818–93) never repeated the success of *Faust*, though *Roméo et Juliette*, which was staged in 1867, eight years after *Faust*, has real charm and *Mireille* is sometimes staged. *Faust*, however, will last as long as opera, for it is full of good tunes including several very famous ones, the Soldier's Chorus, the Jewel Song, the role of Méphistophélès, the Garden Scene, Faust's 'Salut! demeure chaste et pure', Valentine's Prayer, and the emotional finale. It is vital nowadays for it to be cast well for it is not unsinkable.

Ambroise Thomas's *Mignon* (1866) is hard to track down now, though 'Je suis Titania' remains a coloratura showpiece. The original Mignon was a superb artist, Galli-Marié, who was the first *Carmen* in 1875. Georges Bizet (1838–75) died tragically young, too young to see the world-

LEFT
For Berlioz fans (like the author) Les Troyens ranks as one of the greatest of all operas. The complete Trojans (Parts 1 and 2) has recently been produced by the combined forces of Opera North, Welsh National Opera and Scottish Opera. Seen here are Anne Evans as Cassandra and Phillip Joll as Chorebus in the first performance by Welsh National Opera in early 1987. The producer was Tim Albery and the designers Tom Cairns and Antony McDonald.

BELOW
Gounod's Faust was given a new production at Covent Garden in 1974 by John Copley. Here is the garden scene, with Stuart Burrows and Kiri Te Kanawa as the lovers, Heather Begg as Marthe and Norman Treigle as Mephistopheles. As always when well done, the old operatic warhorse triumphed.

Blessed Spirits.' Cassandra is the most striking character in Part I, which has huge scenes and choruses, complete with the Trojan Horse. This is the classical part of the work (for all Berlioz's Romanticism), Part 2 being warmly romantic, passionate and finally tragic. Even Berlioz never equalled elsewhere the great love duet in sheer ecstatic passion, while the spirit of Virgil is never absent.

Béatrice et Bénédict followed, based on Shakespeare's *Much Ado About Nothing*. The score is ravishing but there is far too much spoken dialogue for the average singer to encompass.

BELOW
Agnes Baltsa, the superb Greek mezzo, as Carmen and José Carreras as Don José at Covent Garden in 1986, a high-powered pair in the famous roles.

wide triumph of his *Carmen* (1875). The Parisian scene had improved a little since Berlioz's day, while Bizet himself was less of an outsider. His *Docteur Miracle* (1856–1857) is an entertaining one-act operetta, which was followed by *Don Procopio* (1858–59), and both are enjoyable, both Donizettian. Parts of the forgotten *Ivan IV* were later used in other works. Then came the only opera for which Bizet is remembered apart from *Carmen*.

This is *Les Pêcheurs des Perles* (The Pearl Fishers, 1863). Set in ancient Ceylon, it is very enjoyable and twice rises to the

heights. The tenor's 'Je crois entendre' (I hear as in a dream) is a beautiful inspiration, while the tenor-baritone duet, 'Au fond du temple saint' (In the depths of the temple) is one of the most affectingly beautiful pieces in opera. *La Jolie Fille du Perth* (1867) is a finer work, whose Serenade is often sung; *La Coupe du Roi de Thule* (The Fall of the King of Thule, 1868), followed, much of which is missing and – among others – *Djamileh* (1872). But none of these equal Bizet's magnificent music for Alphonse Daudet's play, *L'Arlésienne*.

Carmen, blessed with a fine libretto by Henri Meilhac and Ludovic Halévy, is the apotheosis of *opéra comique* and is widely regarded as a perfect opera. With so few singers able to speak dialogue convincingly, some prefer to hear Guiraud's recitatives, added six months after the Parisian production when the opera was staged in Vienna.

Carmen's assets are as follows: instantly enjoyable tunes that do not stale; an emotion-charged and excellent story; a brilliantly orchestrated, diamond sharp score, passionate, powerful and amusing; a wealth of well-drawn characters; and local 'colour' which, whether Spaniards like it or not, works stunningly in the opera house. Its famous failure at its premiere was due to many factors. The management began to worry about the plot being unsuitable for their 'family' theatre, the Opéra-Comique, where operas simply did not end with violent death, while the respectable patrons of the theatre did not, it would seem, like to see the heroine's type of friends on stage. There were casting problems as well as financial ones. Marie-Roze, the chosen Carmen, was shocked by the role but, happily, Célestine Galli-Marié, despite doubts about her character, was a true artist. Bizet could not get the ladies of the chorus to behave like cigarette girls, while the first night was postponed for financial reasons. Finally, the masterpiece was staged on 3 March 1875.

It was not the disaster of legend, for the first act went well, but the audience grew colder and many left before the end. The critics disgraced their trade, attacking both the score and the story, calling them undramatic, un-French, un-Spanish, Wagnerian and even unmusical. In fact,

PRECEDING PAGE
Mirella Freni as Micaela in Bizet's ever-popular Carmen, *conducted by Herbert von Karajan. Grace Bumbry sang Carmen and Jon Vickers Don José. The performance is preserved on video.*

the opera stayed in the repertoire for forty-six performances, hardly a failure, but audiences diminished, and Bizet died in June, not knowing that his opera would soon conquer Europe and America – and finally France. That Bizet died disconsolate is a wretched fact. As with Berlioz, the first instinct of the French opera public was to prefer talent to genius.

Camille Saint-Saëns (1835–1921) was no genius, but his *Samson et Dalila* (1877) is a splendid work. Called a near-oratorio, Wagnerian, and, in fact, stately rather than impassioned in parts, it is highly

effective, with two fine roles and one very fine scene when Samson, blind and in chains, turns the mill in Gaza. It is certainly a singers' opera and has always been popular.

Jules Massenet (1842–1912) had a long career and his many operas – he wrote twenty-seven – include some that are in the regular repertoire in France. *Manon* (1884) is his best known, and others include *Hérodiade, Werther, Thaïs, Le Jongleur de Notre-Dame* and *Don Quichotte*. Vincent d'Indy devastatingly noted his 'discreet and semi-religious eroticism',

parisons with Puccini's famous *Manon Lescaut* will be made later.

La Navarraise (1894) is an unjustly neglected opera, while *Le Cid* (1885) has a rare example of true power 'Pleurez, mes yeux'. Those who have heard Callas sing it usually realize that they have underrated this minor master.

Two other such masters were Léo Delibes, whose *Lakmé* contains the famous 'Bell Song' and Edouard Lalo's *Le Roi d'Ys* (1888). Massenet and his contemporaries have to be sought out by operagoers; one place to find a regular supply of 19th-century French works being that delightful annual event, the Wexford Festival.

Some would say that Jacques Offenbach, a German Jewish adopted Frenchman, wrote finer works than most 'serious' French composers. Rossini's tribute has been quoted. Wagner added his – '*Il savait faire comme de divin Mozart*', which may be translated as 'he had the know-how of the divine Mozart.' For all their topicality they can still be enjoyed more than a century after the Second Empire collapsed. *Orphée aux Enfers – Orpheus in the Underworld –* is surely his masterpiece, other rivals to the title being *La Belle Heléne*, *La Vie Parisienne* and *La Périchole*.

LEFT
A scene from English National Opera's Orpheus in the Underworld, *produced by David Pountney with dominating, albeit witty sets by Gerald Scarfe. Downstage is Fiona Kimm as Diana, while Sally Burgess made operatic history by portraying Public Opinion as Mrs. Thatcher with a bustle.*

BELOW
Massenet's Werther *was staged by English National Opera in 1977 with Dame Janet Baker as Charlotte, John Brecknock as Werther and Harold Blackburn as the Magistrate. The conductor was Sir Charles Mackerras, long associated with English National Opera.*

which went down well with audiences who could not take Berlioz in his day. *Manon* has some delightful moments, notably Manon's famous Gavotte in the Cour-la-Reine scene. Stephen Williams noted the composer's 'scented, voluptuous melody', but Massenet could rise to passion, notably in Des Grieux's 'Ah! fuyez, douce image' (Ah! depart, fair image) in *Manon* when he implores the image of Manon to leave him so that he can dedicate himself to the Almighty. Another notable example is the hero's 'Pourquoi me Réveiller' in *Werther*. Com-

Covent Garden's 1980 production of Les Contes d'Hoffman *by Offenbach is a sumptuous affair, produced by film director John Schlesinger and designed by William Dudley and Maria Bjørnson, the latter creating the costumes. The first cast was very starry, including Domingo in the title role and Agnes Baltsa as Guilietta.*

Offenbach's music is tender, uproarious, funny, cynical and sexy, while his orchestration should always be played by a full orchestra. He wrote some ninety operettas. Only a time machine, however, could give us the extra pleasure of topicality, one extreme example being the first night of *La Grande Duchess de Gérolstein* in 1867, with Bismarck in the audience watching himself being parodied on stage – and knowing that soon he would topple the Emperor Napoleon III and his whole pleasure-mad capital.

Offenbach lost favour in the aftermath of the Franco-Prussian War, but he had one more ace up his sleeve, *Les Contes d'Hoffmann* (The Tales of Hoffmann) produced some months after he had died in 1881. It is dazzling entertainment, an extravagant, romantic box of tricks, with a prologue and three contrasting scenes, and it has never been out of the international repertoire. Offenbach's legion of admirers long for a time when more and more of his operettas enjoy that blessed state.

CHAPTER SIX

Nationalism and Realism

'Nationalism' in opera is a suspect concept. It is there but must be viewed with suspicion. Like concertgoers, opera-lovers hear nationalist sounds because they are often led to expect them. A notorious example in orchestral music is the slow movement of the New World Symphony by Dvořák. 'Everyone' knows it is an American melody, but it is not. It is a Czech tune, the composition of a home-sick exile, which was turned into a Negro spiritual, *Goin' Home*.

There are, of course, dance rhythms and turns of musical phrases that are nationalist in that they proclaim Spain, Russia, Hungary, etc. Bizet added Spanish 'colour' to his 'French' music for *Carmen*. Verdi's *Don Carlos* has a 'Spanish' Veil Song. In fact, the Italian Verdi, using a shortened version of a German play, recreated Philip II's Spain in his musical imagination. However nations do have characteristic 'sounds' at certain periods. The Russians resented Italian influence and founded their own school of Russian music in the mid-19th century, the culmination of which was Mussorgsky's *Boris Godunov*. Verdi visited Russia in 1862, the patriotic Italian upsetting patriotic Russians, and getting paid a lot of roubles.

Happily, the result was a Russian explosion of talent. Italians and French had dominated the Imperial Opera at the capital, St. Petersburg, but Russian composers, albeit copying Italian models at first, prepared the way for future developments. Alexis Verstovsky (1799–1862), an admirer of *Der Freischütz*, tried to found a Russian school but it was Mikhail Glinka (1804–57) who succeeded. His *A Life for the Tsar* (1836), now called *Ivan Susanin*, is the corner stone of Russian opera, especially in its choral scenes. Others show Italian influence. *Ruslan and Ludmila* (1842) was even more Russian, a

fairy-tale still given today. Alexander Dargomizhsky (1813–69) wrote *Rusalka* – as did Dvořák – and, more significantly, *The Stone Guest* (1872), a Don Giovanni opera of no great merit but one that used the inflections of Russian speech.

Then came 'The Five' – known as 'The Mighty Handful', who inherited Glinka's mission, Balakirev, Borodin, Cui, Rimsky-Korsakov and, above all, Mussorgsky. These led the fight to purge Russian music of Western tendencies.

Tchaikovsky's splendid The Queen of Spades was staged by English National Opera in 1983 with Sarah Walker as the aged Countess and Graham Clark as Hermann, the young officer desperate to find the secret of winning at cards. David Pountney produced, Mark Elder conducted and Maria Bjørnson was the designer.

Mussorgsky (1839–81) was an ex-guards officer who became an alcoholic and died of epilepsy. He created the greatest masterpiece in Russian music, *Boris Godunov* (1874), with two heroes, the guilty Tsar who has murdered to get the Crown, and the Russian people.

The libretto is based on Pushkin's historical drama and is totally linked to the Russian language. The sound he unleashed was gloriously free, passionate, monumental and moving with glorious choral moments. His orchestration – now used often in the West – was stark, so much so that Rimsky-Korsakov rescored and revised the opera after the composer's death to make it acceptable. The masterpiece became world famous when the supreme actor-singer, Feodor Chaliapin (1873–1938) made the title-role his own. Yet however it is given the effect is overwhelming. Mussorgsky's other masterpiece is the unfinished *Khovanshchina*, a sprawling piece set in the 17th century, full of magnificent music, while his comedy *Sorochintsy Fair* comes from a Gogol story.

Rimsky-Korsakov, the master orchestrator, is in a lesser league because his operas lack drama and ordinary human feelings, but they are fine and spectacular entertainments. They include *The Tsar's Bride*, *The Snow Maiden* and *The Golden Cockerel*. His *Sadko* has a 'Song of the Viking Guest' so thrilling that it makes one sigh for what he might have achieved. He also had a hand in Borodin's *Prince Igor*, whose finest section is the Polovtsian Dances.

Peter Tchaikovsky (1840–93) did not neglect the West and bridges the two cultures, most notably in two masterpieces, *Eugene Onegin* (1879) and *The Queen of Spades* (1890), both from Pushkin. His other operas include the delightful *Cherevichi* (The Little Shoes, 1886) and the powerful and melodic *Mazeppa* (1884). None equal *Onegin*, whose heroine Tatiana is one of the most attractive characters in opera. Her Letter Scene in which she writes of her love to the Byronic hero, is a supreme creation. *The Queen of Spades* is melodramatic compared with *Onegin*, but none the worse for that, and the aged Countess is a superb creation. The heroine Lisa commits suicide in the Neva River, but fortunately

sings a glorious aria before doing so. Tchaikovsky's operas are greatly loved in Russia and regularly performed.

Czechoslovakia is a most operatic country but few Czech operas travelled well until the recent happy upsurge in Janáček's popularity. He belongs to a later chapter, but Smetana and Dvořák must be considered here. Bedřich Smetana (1824–84) was known for many years outside his country, then Bohemia, simply by *The Bartered Bride* (1866), an opera of universal appeal. *The Brandenburgers in Bohemia* (1866) is a patriotic work not often seen abroad, but *Dalibor* (1868) has exported well. It is a rescue opera of heroic proportions. Other works include the entertaining *The Two Widows*, *The Kiss* and *The Secret*. Antonin Dvořák (1841–1904), popular in the concert hall, has not travelled so well operatically, except for his hauntingly beautiful *Rusalka* (1901). The

Welsh National Opera's 1982 production of Smetana's masterpiece, The Bartered Bride. *The action was set in the village inn by producer Rudolf Noelte. Helen Field was excellent as Marenka.*

Czechs also enjoy *The Pig-headed Peasants*, *The Jacobin* and *The Peasant a Rogue*. *Dimitrij* is about Boris Godunov's usurper.

Spain, though appreciating opera, has few works known outside its borders. However, Italian opera has always been popular there and *zarzuelas*, wide-ranging and sometimes satirical comic operas, have wide appeal.

Poland's one famous opera is *Halka* (1858) by Stanislaw Moniuszko (1899–72) a Romantic work that is basically Italian in style with Polish colour added. Later operas include Karol Szymanowski's fine romantic *Hagith* (1922) and *King Roger* (1926).

Italian influence spread to Sweden and Hungary, but national voices were heard, in Ivar Hallstrom's *The Enchanted Cat* and *The Bewitched One*, and in the Hungarian Ferenc Erkel's *Bánk Bán* of 1861, a patriotic piece similar to Verdi's blazing epics.

Britain had more opera than is generally realized in the 19th century, though not much creative talent. Italian opera was in great demand at the Royal Italian Opera (now Covent Garden), the language serving French and German operas there for much of the century. There were a number of touring opera companies, but despite many premieres (tracked down by Eric Walter White in his *The Rise of English Opera*) few operas which are even remembered by name. These are remembered, Michael Balfe's *The Bohemian Girl* (1843), *Maritana* by Vincent Wallace (1845) and Sir Julius Benedict's *The Lily of Killarney* (1862). Later came Sir Arthur Sullivan's *Ivanhoe* (1891), minus Gilbert. It was meant to start an English National Opera at the Palace Theatre. The time would come.

It did not help that most of the English establishment was anti-opera, except perhaps the German variety. Fortunately Queen Victoria adored it, even taking Wagner in her stride before he was world famous. The British backed Gilbert and Sullivan, as did many Americans.

The original D'Oyly Carte company was a strong one. Sullivan was a fine musician and tunesmith, and Gilbert, for all his puns, a witty man of the theatre. With Richard D'Oyly Carte managing the company with great flair and efficiency,

they gave Britain a stream of operettas, most of which are still loved. Sullivan's reputation has soared since his music has been played by symphony orchestras, while Gilbert provided and provides much entertainment. Their partnership began in 1871 and ended in 1896, their famous and worst quarrel taking place during the run of *The Gondoliers*. Sex, as opposed to romance, is not present in their operas, but they conquered the Anglo-American world, their most popular piece perhaps being *The Mikado* (1885), the most ravishing score – perhaps again – being for *Iolanthe* (1882).

Native American opera was rare in America in the last century but opera there was, long before the Metropolitan Opera opened its doors in 1883, indeed ballad operas were staged before the Revolution. New York's real baptism came in 1825, the García family giving *The Barber of Seville* with the sixteen-year-old Maria García (later Malibran) as Rosina. There was Italian opera in gold rush California from 1852; but despite the inspiration of touring companies, not much in the way of native operas until this century. America's chief contribution to opera has been singers rather than composers. Meanwhile Argentina has had opera since the 1820s and Mexico, as well as imported

A scene from David Pountney's controversial production of Dvořák's Rusalka, with Eilene Hannan (centre) on the rostrum giving a superb performance and Jane Eaglen (left) as the Foreign Princess. The designer was Stefanos Lazaridis. This was a revival in 1986 of the 1983 production.

zarzuelas, operas of its own. The first truly Mexican opera on a Mexican historical theme was Aniceto Ortega's *Guatimotzin* in 1871.

No account of opera can neglect Viennese operetta. Offenbach's successes in Vienna spurred on native talent. Johann Strauss the Younger (1825–99) was a famous Waltz King long before his success in operetta. His masterpiece *Die Fledermaus* (The Bat, 1874) has been hugely popular for more than a century, its potent blend of tunes, charm, orchestration, champagne and high spirits combining to make a masterpiece. It deserves really fine singing, though only a terrible cast could sink it utterly. It was Offenbach who steered Strauss towards operetta. *Fledermaus's* many joys include Adele's 'Mein Herr Marquis', Rosalinda's tremendous mock *czardas* (she's masquerading as a Hungarian!) and the strange but captivating song Prince Orlofsky (a mezzo) sings, 'Chacun à son goût' (Everyone to his own taste). There is also a toast to King Champagne.

Strauss's other triumphs included *Der Zigeunerbaron* (The Gypsy Baron, 1885) and *Eine Nacht in Venedig* (A Night in Venice, 1883). Franz von Suppé (1819–95) was not the equal of Strauss, but all too rare chances to catch his works must be taken. *Boccaccio* (1879) is the best known. The third giant was Karl Millöcker (1842–99), whose best-known work is *Der Bettelstudent* (The Beggar Student, 1882). Other composers of operettas which have lasted are Richard Genée and Karl Zeller, the latter's *Der Vogelhändler* (The Birdseller) and *Der Obersteiger* (The Master-miner) having been performed far beyond Austria. As for Franz Lehár, his story belongs later, when he rescued what seemed a dead form from oblivion.

Realism, when considering a performing art, is a word to be used with reservations. Even a realistic film is not 'the real thing'. Yet like Romanticism and Nationalism, the word is useful enough as long as its limitations are realized, especially when applied to the arts of opera and ballet. This must be stressed as we have reached the school of Italian *verismo,* which began with Mascagni and culminated in the operas of Puccini. Some 'authorities' who

should know better have claimed that *verismo* portrays the seamy side of life, which is untrue: it portrays all sides of life. It simply means Realism, or Naturalism, both of them loaded words. Suggestion is all. War films do not show actual deaths and distintegrating bodies, nor *verismo* operas actual blood, accidents apart.

Carmen has already been discussed and suggested as the first *verismo* opera, but *verismo* proper begins with Pietro Mascagni (1863–1945). He left the Milan Conservatory early to learn his trade as a

conductor of one of the very many companies touring Italy a century ago. Realism was already part of European
literature – Emile Zola being one exponent of it – and it was bound to happen
that opera would take it up in contrast to
the works of Wagner and Verdi. Yet at
once the word contrast becomes suspect,
because the very romantic *La Traviata* is
also, by operatic standards, realistic except when blown up to admittedly striking proportions in Franco Zeffirelli's film.

It was Mascagni's *Cavalleria Rusticana*

(Rustic Chivalry, 1890) that set off the
Italian *verismo* explosion. Its librettists,
Giovanni Targioni-Tozzetti and Guido
Menasci, took their story from Giovanni
Verga's very popular play of the same
name. Adored by all except the austere, it
has a primitive strength and directness
added to its powerful melodies which
hold most audiences in a vice-like grip. It
conquered Europe and remains a perfect
example of the first class second rate in
art. It does not aspire to the musical
heights of its 'terrible twin' *I Pagliacci* but,

A merry line-up in Die Fledermaus at Covent Garden in 1984. From left to right: Michael Langdon, Doris Soffel, Kiri Te Kanawa, Hermann Prey, Benjamin Luxon and Hildegard Heichele.

in the author's experience, it is even more popular.

Mascagni could never repeat his success, though L'Amico Fritz (1891) is still very popular in Italy. It possesses an intermezzo that deserves to be as popular as Cavalleria's. His Iris (1898) is sometimes revived and Il Picolo Marat (1921) is said to contain his best music. He ended his life under a cloud because of Mussolini's patronage.

Ruggiero Leoncavallo (1858–1919) is remembered almost solely for Pagliacci (The Clowns, 1892). It is based on an incident in his father's life. He was a judge and had to try a jealous actor who had murdered his wife during a performance. The result was a marvellously dramatic opera from the start with its famous Prologue to the famous ending – 'La commedia e finito'.

These two simple masterpieces make an excellent introduction to opera for newcomers. Double and triple bills, often seen in ballet, are not usually popular with opera audiences, but Cav and Pag in tandem will last as long as opera does.

For the record, Leoncavallo also com-

(still) the most famous of all tenors.

Umberto Giordano (1867–1948) wrote ten operas, only one of which is still widely loved in Italy, his French Revolutionary opera *Andrea Chénier*, based on the life of the poet who was guillotined. Puritanical Anglo-Saxon critics sneer at it; audiences who know a fine second-rate work when they hear and see it will always respond to it when presented with the right cast. One moment is truly great, the hero's impassioned *Improvviso*, an intoxicating explosion of revolutionary fervour, while the last, short act is a splendid one ending with hero and heroine bound for the guillotine. In Italy at least Giordano's *Fedora* (1898), set in Tsarist Russia, is still heard, its hero being an aristocratic nihilist who loves a princess.

Another minor master, Francesco Cilèa (1866–1950) wrote *L'Arlesiana* (1897) with its lyrical 'Lamento di Federico', and the still-performed *Adriana Lecouvreur* (1902) taken from a play by Eugène Scribe and Ernest Legouvé about the famous 18th-century actress and her love affair with Marshal de Saxe. When it was staged at the Camden Festival in 1972 most London critics were outraged at having to sit through it. Most operagoers, however, were delighted to hear a modest but effective work.

Only a half century ago the great Puccini, too, was sending some English

Zeffirelli on the set of Cavalleria Rusticana which was filmed in Sicily and at La Scala.

posed a *La Bohème* (1897) which is a skilled and enjoyable piece, and which has Marcello and Musetta as the important couple, not Mimi and Rodolfo. It was bad luck for him that Puccini made the subject his own. His earliest pieces, *Chatterton* and *I Medici*, were to be part of a trilogy, but he gave up when the latter failed. His *Zaza* (1900) can be found by avid searchers from time to time. Yet it was his *Vesti la giubba* (On with the Motley) from *Pagliacci* which was the first to achieve a million sales, as sung by the great Caruso, albeit in several different recordings by

critics into frenzies of disdain. The usually admirable librettist, teacher and writer, Edward J. Dent, deeply distressed many of the composer's admirers by using the phrase 'slobbering erotics' about the master and accusing him of writing arias to fit on records. Other less drastic scribes, while allowing him some theatrical skill, a matter of importance in opera after all, could scarcely conceal their contemptuous feelings. The majority of opera lovers fell in love with his music, Sir Thomas Beecham making the point that to the average man Puccini *was* opera. It was true early in this century before Verdi's star in Britain reached heights from which it will never depart.

Giacomo Puccini (1858–1924) came from a line of musicians. Born in Lucca, he studied under Ponchielli in Milan. Though Puccini did not achieve international fame until he was in his mid-thirties, once he had attained it he became the only composer since Verdi and

Another amusing cartoon by Caruso, this one a picture of Puccini in 1910, the year La Fanciulla del West *was staged in New York, with the opera's heroine Minnie under his arm.*

LEFT
Kiri Te Kanawa and Placido Domingo in the embarkation scene at Le Havre in Puccini's first masterpiece, Manon Lescaut. *Produced in 1983 at The Royal Opera House, Covent Garden, by Götz Friedrich, this timeless classic was made into a video with the original cast and conducted by Giuseppe Sinopoli.*

OPPOSITE
Franco Zeffirelli's production of Pagliacci *at La Scala with Domingo, Teresa Stratas and Juan Pons. Georges Prêtre was the conductor.*

Wagner to make a large contribution to the regular operatic repertoire, certainly a larger one than Richard Strauss.

He was never so much a *verismo* composer as Mascagni. A more romantic glow shines over his Bohemians than a hard-core *verismo* composer would have allowed. He was Verdi's true successor even though in his maturity he never tried to emulate the grandeur of Verdi's themes: epic love, heroism, patriotism, honour. He could have composed a Traviata opera and, so *Gianni Schicchi* suggests, a Falstaff one, but he wisely never tried to adventure into the surging worlds of *Rigoletto*, *Simon Boccanegra* and *Otello*. That said, the grandeur of *Turandot* comes to mind, yet then one recalls that the opera's most vivid character is Liu, the last of his line of 'little women'.

The composer lived in a less far-ranging world than Verdi, one suited to his lesser but extraordinary gifts. His flair for melody – lyrical, sensuous, striking and beguiling was supported by masterly orchestration and tremendous theatrical flair. He listened to his contemporaries and, without blurring his fingerprints, learnt from them: Debussyan harmonies in *La Fanciulla del West* and a neo-Stravinskyan passage in *Gianni Schicchi*. Verdi influenced him but so did Wagner, not least in his use of the *leitmotiv*, while the magnificent opening act of *Turandot* has choral music that calls to mind the crowd scenes of *Boris Godunov*. Yet Puccini created his own unique world.

His first opera, *Le Villi* (The Witches, 1884) is a one-acter which had Verdi worrying about the young man's symphonic tendencies. Unlike *Edgar* (1889) it was a success. *Edgar* showed he had not yet discovered his operatic identity, but the publishing house of Ricordi believed in him and was rewarded with his first great success, *Manon Lescaut* (1893). It does not supplant Massenet's *Manon*, but is more full-blooded, with a succession of fresh, often overwhelming melodies. The third act on the quay at Le Havre shows genius, the rest is beyond mere talent. When the tragic lovers are portrayed by great artists – Domingo and Kiri Te Kanawa spring to mind – the effect is overwhelming, the last act rising to tragic grandeur.

The Bulgarian soprano, Raina Kabaivanska, a beautiful actress-singer, as Madama Butterfly at the Arena di Verona in 1983. Her Pinkerton was Nazzareno Antinori.

OPPOSITE TOP
La Bohème was revived at Covent Garden in 1982, John Copley's 1974 production and Julia Trevelyan Oman's sets being as satisfying as ever. The voices on this occasion blended beautifully: Ileana Cotrubas as Mimi, Neil Shicoff as Rodolfo, Marilyn Zschau as Musetta and Thomas Allen as Marcello, with Gwynne Howell as Colline. Lamberto Gardelli was the experienced and excellent conductor.

OPPOSITE BOTTOM
Giacomo Aragall as Cavaradossi and Eva Marton as Tosca, respectively from Spain and Hungary, in Tosca at the Arena di Verona in 1984.

113

Puccini was never to have such a total triumph for a new opera again. It took place eight days before the first *Falstaff* and rapidly went round the operatic world. Bernard Shaw hailed Puccini as Verdi's successor.

Even non-Puccinians appear to enjoy *La Bohème* (1896). The libretto, by Guiseppe Giacosa and Luigi Illica after Murger's novel, is a good one and helped him reach maturity and mastery. The opera varies between fast action and radiant lyricism. It is fresh and beautifully crafted, a hymn to youth which captivates young and old. The beginning with its swift opening and the famous love scene; the kaleidoscopic excitement and tunefulness of Act II; the surging lyricism of the third act; the happy horseplay of the final act that turns to tragedy, all ensure that only a very poor performance can spoil Puccini's magic. Toscanini was in the pit

and theatrical impact is immense, and occasionally it gets a historic production, the most famous being at Covent Garden in 1964 by Zeffirelli, with Callas and Gobbi giving performances in Act II that achieved instant immortality. On this occasion *Tosca* truly shocked. Puccini admitted that he had coloured the drama from without rather than illuminating it from within, but audiences respond overwhelmingly to what they have. The critics were unfriendly – especially about the libretto, rivals were said to be fomenting trouble, but *Tosca* soon swept the operatic world. The first night of *Madama Butterfly* in 1904 was an even greater disaster, jealous wreckers being at work. Puccini had seen David Belasco's play and knew it was right for him. He did revise the opera somewhat after the débâcle, but the first version was excellent, as could been seen when the Welsh National Opera staged it. Three months after the Scala failure it triumphed at Brescia, and this third and last total success was truly launched.

The opera is a true tragedy, not a melodrama, Butterfly being Puccini's ultimate 'little woman'. Some genuine Japanese tunes are used and the oriental atmosphere is right. Butterfly's development is finely done and the final scene found the composer excelling himself. Belasco's play and John Luther Long's original story are forgotten; the opera is adored.

Another magnificent work followed, *La Fanciulla del West* (The Girl of the

at the premiere in Turin. The critics failed to recognize a winner and failed again in Rome, along with audiences. Then came Palermo and the conquest of the world began. It is being given every night of the year in one or more places and always will be while opera lasts.

Tosca, called by the puritanical critic, Joseph Kerman, in his *Opera as Drama*, a 'shabby little shocker', is less moving than *Bohème* and more *verismo*. Its musical

ABOVE
Gustave Charpentier's
Louise *was very popular
in the early years of the
century but is rarely staged
today. English National
Opera produced it in
1980. The heroine, like
Mimi in* La Bohème, *is a
seamstress. Some say that
the true heroine of the
opera is Paris. The
production by Colin
Graham gave Valerie
Masterson another chance
to excel in French opera.
She appears here with
John Treleaven.*

OPPOSITE
*Gwyneth Jones as
Turandot and Placido
Domingo as Calaf in the
1984 Covent Garden
production of* Turandot,
*which had its premiere at
Los Angeles.*

lesser work, but Angelica has such fine music that managements who leave the opera out of the *Trittico* deserve some operatic fate. The third, *Gianni Schicchi* is adored by musicians and critics – and, one may assume, by everyone else. It is funny and has a host of Florentine characters, being based on Dante. 'O mio babbino caro' (O my beloved daddy) shows us the composer ravishingly satirizing himself.

Puccini's last opera was staged after his death. This was *Turandot*, his grandest opera, finished by Franco Alfano because Puccini died in 1924 before he had completed it. It is a black fable set in Peking, with an icy princess as the anti-heroine who sends would-be lovers to their deaths if they cannot answer her three riddles. Calaf solves them but his adoring Liu, who has some bewitching music, kills herself rather than reveal who Calaf is to the Princess. Liu's music is as touching as anything he ever composed. Puccini was obliged to stop work on the score after completing her death scene. Toscanini conducted the premiere at La Scala in 1926, finishing the opera where Puccini put down his pen. He spoke a few broken words and the performance ended. The next evening Alfano's honest efforts were heard. They get the curtain down adequately, but the mystery remains as to how Puccini would have ended his grandest opera with its ice-cold, cruel heroine. And with that glorious score, its choruses grandly inspired by the influence of *Boris Godunov*, its music ravishingly lyrical as well as powerful, the great line of Italian composers of opera came to an end.

Golden West, 1910) from a Belasco play about the California gold rush. Puccini buffs used to have to defend the work – not the magnificent music – until 1977 when Covent Garden staged a marvel of a production by Piero Faggioni with realistic designs by Ken Adam, with Zubin Mehta in the pit and Carol Neblett, Placido Domingo and Silvano Carroli as the principals, which was a runaway hit and a triumph for Puccini and all concerned. The opera has a happy, 'not-a-dry-eye-in-the-house' ending, which makes a change.

La Rondine (1917), dubbed a 'poor-man's Traviata', lies between opera and operetta and is entertaining and tuneful with good crowd scenes, but it is not a major work. His *Trittico* (1918), three one-act operas, is a different matter. *Il Tabarro*, set on a Seine barge and on the river bank, is a short *verismo* masterpiece with a superbly atmospheric score and a host of well-drawn characters. The three principals are a jealous, suspicious husband, his unfaithful wife, and her lover; a Grand Guignol story which is both passionate and believable. *Suor Angelica*, set in a convent – Puccini had a sister in one – is a

A few non-Italians used *verismo*, very few of them Germans, though Eugen d'Albert's *Tiefland* (1903) is a popular example. Of his other twenty operas only *Die Abreise* (The Departure, 1898), a comedy written before *verismo* beckoned him, is occasionally staged. *Louise* (1900) by Gustave Charpentier (1860–1956) is a notable French *verismo* opera, and some say *Carmen* is another. *Louise* is a delightful opera, once widely given, though now rarely outside France. 'Depuis le jour' is its best-known aria, while the heroine has a rival in the city of Paris, which the composer paints with notable skill.

CHAPTER SEVEN

The World of Richard Strauss

Savagely and unfairly attacked by Ken Russell in a TV film, and characterized most unflatteringly by Mahler's widow, Richard Strauss (1864–1949) was the last of a line of great German composers. Professional singers and orchestral players liked working with him – always a good sign. In 1945 his street was liberated by American soldiers, but he wondered how he could introduce himself to them. The tall stooping old man put his hand

out to the officer and said: 'I am the composer of *Der Rosenkavalier*.' The officer knew it, as well he might, for it is more loved than any other German opera since Mozart's day. Dedicated Straussians may have other favourites, but like nearly all operagoers they love *Rosenkavalier*.

With Strauss's death we reach the end of a line. He was the last of the giants, while *Rosenkavalier* inhabits a pantheon that contains four Mozart operas, three of Puccini's, slightly more Verdi ones and very few others. Modern opera will be covered later, but not at the expense of operas that fill seats all over the world. By that token Strauss was the last of the elect.

The son of a famous horn player, Strauss made his first reputation as a conductor. His *Guntram* (1894) and *Feuersnot* (Beltane Fire, 1900) were not surprisingly influenced by Wagner, with hints in the latter of glory to come. *Salome* (1905) from Oscar Wilde's play, made him famous and controversial. Powerful, violent, claustrophobically sensual, it is a superb score though some find parts of it sickly sweet. It is in one act and the casting of the heroine is vital – and not easy, for the soprano has to convince as a nubile sixteen-year-old with the voice of a Brünnhilde or an Isolde. Strauss adored the soprano voice, but he was no easy taskmaster, expecting his Salome to perform the Dance of the Seven Veils. Grace Bumbry, Gwyneth Jones and Josephine Barstow are among those who have lately succeeded. They did not have Strauss at rehearsals shouting: 'Louder! I can still hear the singers!' One hopes this was teasing. Once he told the players to play *Salome* as if it was fairy music.

Elektra (1909) saw him collaborating with the poet and dramatist Hugo von Hofmannsthal for the first time. It is a finer, fiercer work than *Salome*, the characters more brilliantly drawn, the music drama, again in a single act, truly tragic. A simple shattering *leitmotiv* – that of the murdered Agammemnon – towers over the work. The scene between Elektra and Klytemnestra is beyond anything in *Salome* psychologically, the music is as frightening as a snake pit. The orchestra numbers 115 players and several hearings are needed to unravel the great score's secrets. Only the music for Elektra's exultant frenzied dance of death, when her mother has been

LEFT
Yvonne Minton as Octavian and Yvonne Kenney as Sophie in Richard Strauss's Der Rosenkavalier *at Covent Garden in 1983. Gwyneth Jones was the Marschallin. This much-loved work is rarely out of the Covent Garden repertoire for long, and is, world-wide, the composer's most popular opera.*

119

killed along with her love, has been challenged by some. The individual must decide. Few modern works sound so modern as this cataclysmic outpouring.

Der Rosenkavalier (The Knight of the Rose, 1911) is totally different and has been adored since its premiere in Dresden. In the aftermath of the First World War it became a symbol of vanished beauty, partly because the final radiant trio has an almost unbearable quality, which evokes loss as well as love. Hofmannsthal again contributed to its success. Luscious as the music is, its simplicity captivates the heart at certain moments, such as in the presentation of the rose by Octavian to Sophie. Strauss deliberately and anachronistically used 19th-century waltzes for his 18th-century story. The four leading roles, the third being the legendary one of the Feldmarschallin, experienced and sophisticated, the fourth the boorish Baron Ochs, are all wonderfully drawn. Octavian, the young knight who bears the rose to Sophie, is sung by a mezzo (Strauss's obsession with the female voice never ended) which makes the opening scene – after love-making has been heard in the prelude – somewhat startling to newcomers to the opera. Yet Octavian is seventeen and no tenor of that age could sing such a role. Hopefully, the newcomer to opera will get the right cast and worries will vanish. Not to succumb to *Der Rosenkavalier* is to miss a great musical experience.

Ariadne auf Naxos followed in 1912, the opera being preceded by a performance of Molière's *Le Bourgeois Gentilhomme*. This is sometimes performed but, naturally, the cost of actors as well as singers was and is a serious matter, so Strauss and his colleague created a second version, with the gentleman of the house hiring an opera troupe and *commedia dell'arte* players. Composer and librettist worked a miracle and created a masterpiece, the gentleman of the house demanding that *both* shows must be played simultaneously. The result is enchanting. The Composer in the second version, distraught but enchanted, is a major creation (again, for a soprano), Zerbinetta of the *commedia* troupe has one of the most taxing coloratura arias ever conceived, while Bacchus and Ariadne in

LEFT
Leonie Rysanek (left) as Elektra with Astrid Varnay in her remarkable role of Klytemnestra. This was a powerful production of Richard Strauss's Elektra by Götz Friedrich.

OVERLEAF
The famous Presentation of the Rose scene – a silver rose borne to Sophie by the Rosenkavalier in the second act of Der Rosenkavalier. *The pair fall in love, which is not meant to happen, presenting Strauss with an opportunity to provide sumptuous music.*

121

LEFT
*Lucia Popp (left) and
Marie McLaughlin in
Act III of Richard
Strauss's* Arabella *at
Covent Garden in 1986,
a welcome revival expertly
conducted by Bernard
Haitink. It also featured
Bernd Weikl as
Mandryka, Helga
Dernesch as Adelaide and
Walter Berry as Waldner.*

BELOW
A new Ariadne auf
Naxos *(Richard Strauss)
was presented at Covent
Garden in 1985,
produced by Jean-Louis
Martinoty and conducted
by Jeffrey Tate. Seen here
are Jessye Norman as
Ariadne and Kathleen
Battle as Zerbinetta.*

the serious part of the entertainment have a miraculous duet (in both versions). Bacchus, it must be noted, is a tenor, not a soprano.

Die Frau ohne Schatten followed in 1919, Hofmannsthal aiming at a complicated allegory. 'Schatten' means shadow and the Empress has none, symbolizing the fact that she is childless. Some rate it as the composer's masterpiece, others do not. Barak the dyer has some of the warmest music, a fine man with radiant music to prove his goodness; not the easiest thing for a composer, but Strauss achieves it. Some of the most heart-warming German music since *Meistersinger* is heard when watchmen sing a hymn in the street urging couples to love one another. As the curtain falls on Act II Barak lies down to rest alone, for his shrewish wife will not love him. The opera ends happily.

Intermezzo (1924) is a two-act delight based on a misunderstanding between the Strausses, and when first staged at Dresden the husband and wife looked just like the composer and his wife. *Die Ägyptische Helena* (The Egyptian Helen 1928) has fine music but is dramatically feeble. Its love scene is magnificent. *Arabella* (1933) was Strauss's last work with his great librettist and is an enchanting Viennese comedy, only marginally inferior to *Der Rosenkavalier*. Lila della Casa is the most famous of all Arabellas while the forthright Mandryka is also a fine role.

123

There followed *Die schweigsame Frau* (The Silent Woman, 1935) from Ben Jonson's comedy *Epicoene*, amusing enough, but musically underpowered; *Friedenstag* (The Day of Peace, 1938) a one act historical drama; *Dafne*, a bucolic drama according to the librettist Josef Gregor, and *Die Liebe der Danae* (1938–40, produced 1952) with glorious music but a mythological libretto by Gregor that was below standard. Strauss was adored by orchestral players and the 'rain of gold' sequence in the opera was yet another example of why they adored him. His final opera was *Capriccio* (1942), in one long scene lasting two and a half hours and dramatizing the problem of words and music in opera in a delightful and successful way. The libretto was by the composer and Clemens Krauss, the conductor at the premiere.

Strauss's immortality is secure. Petty arguments and criticisms are beside the point and indeed unfair. He was accused of liking to make money, but most artists want to do so, having their feet firmly on the ground. *Salome, Elektra, Rosenkavalier, Ariadne* – and surely *Die Frau ohne Schatten* – will ensure his operatic immortality. His love affair with the human voice ended in his *Four Last Songs*, his final tribute to the soprano voice he loved so well.

When Richard Strauss was at the height of his powers no one can have guessed that, soon, new operas would not find a public. Puccini, too, was surely preparing the way for new Italian glories, while in France Debussy was making musical history.

Claude Debussy (1862–1918) certainly advanced the frontiers of opera, but his single work, *Pelléas et Mélisande* (1902), is a lonely masterpiece. Some have said it is part of the Romantic Movement, but it has also been called the masterpiece of modern impressionist French music.

Its Wagnerian interludes carry much of the opera's emotions, but *Pelléas* is as restrained as Wagner is not. Despite its passionate plot, taken from Maurice Maeterlinck's Symbolist play, a tale of jealousy and murder, Debussy chooses subtlety and extreme understatement. The world he creates is a twilight one, a phantom-like version of Tristan and Isolde's world. Debussy presented crystal clear recitative and followed natural speech. The characters are not vividly drawn, the drama is hardly strong, for all the felicities in the score. It therefore attracts passionate support or bored hostility. Debussy, a musical giant, therefore did not start a school of opera, though many composers were inspired by him, including Puccini in parts of *Fanciulla*.

Strauss lovers are divided about the merits of Die Frau ohne Schatten (The Woman Without a Shadow), *which many consider a masterpiece. Here is Welsh National Opera's production by Gilbert Deflo, with Richard Armstrong conducting. The whole enterprise was a credit to the company. Anne Evans was the Empress, Pauline Tinsley, the Dyer's Wife, Matti Kastu, the Emperor, Patricia Payne, the Nurse and Norman Bailey, Barak.*

Debussy's masterpiece, Pelléas et Mélisande, was produced by Vaclav Kaslik at Covent Garden in 1969, with striking scenery by Josef Svoboda. Elisabeth Söderstrom was memorable as the heroine, and George Shirley was a fine Pelléas. Pierre Boulez conducted.

125

CHAPTER EIGHT

Yesterday, Today and Tomorrow

RIGHT
Riccardo Zandonai's
Francesca da Rimini *was
given a sumptuous
production at New York's
Metropolitan Opera by
Franco Zeffirelli in 1984.
Domingo was the hero,
Paolo, and Renata Scotto
the heroine, Francesca,
with Cornell MacNeil as
a splendid villain. Too
expensive for most houses
to stage – it has to be
staged expensively or not
at all – it was a
marvellous event,
fortunately captured on
video.*

The young in the arts understandably attack their elders, wanting to promote their own beliefs. Yet they are rarely as savage as those Italian musicians who attacked the *verismo* composers, especially Puccini. Some attacks were sheer jealousy, others were idealistic. Puccini's artistic integrity was admirable, but it did not necessarily seem so to the next generation.

Those composers who stayed true to tradition and to *verismo*, benefited from musical advances elsewhere. The most gifted was Riccardo Zandonai (1883–1944). His operas include the successful *Conchita* (1911) and the triumphant *Francesca da Rimini* (1914). Those who saw the New York Metropolitan's sumptuous production by Zeffirelli, which was televised, will know that the opera 'works' but without Puccini's melodic and dramatic thrust and genius. He also wrote *Giuletta e Romeo* and *I Cavalieri di Ekubu*, and he is not forgotten in his native country. Italo Montemezzi (1875–1952) was more a disciple of Boito than a *verismo* composer. He triumphed with *Giovanni Gallurese* (1905), his first opera, his later works, including his finest, *L'Amore dei tre Re* (1913) were more successful abroad than in Italy.

Best known for his orchestra scene-painting, Ottorino Respighi (1879–1936) was an anti-*verismo* composer. His work was influenced by German and old Italian trends and lacks drama – something the *verismo* school could never be charged with – yet they are richly scored. They include *Belfagor* (1923) and *La Fiamma* (The Flame 1934), this last enjoying much success in Italy.

Gian Francesco Malipiero (1882–1973) championed ancient Italian music, his operas including *Giulio Cesare* (1936), but better known outside Italy is Ildebrando

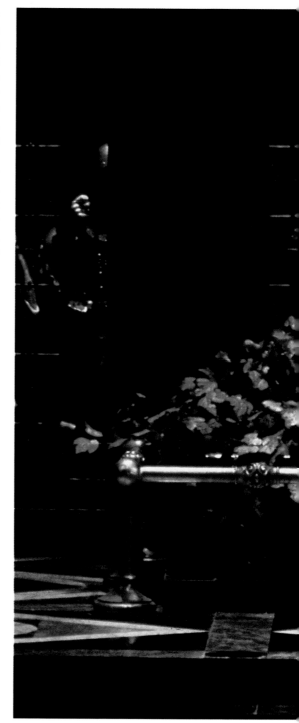

Pizzetti (1880–1968) whose successes include *Debora e Jaele* (1922) and *L'Assassinio nella Cattedrale* (1961) from T.S. Eliot's Becket play, *Murder in the Cathedral*.

These respectable composers may or may not survive the test of time, but Gian Carlo Menotti (1911–), an American of Italian birth, and the founder of the Festival of Two Worlds at Spoleto, may do so despite savage attacks on his works.

In the 1940s he wrote *The Telephone* and *The Medium*, both efficient and entertaining, while *The Consul* (1950), though abused for its allegedly sub-Puccinian music, was a fine piece of music-theatre. His *Amahl and the Night Visitors* (1951) is a Christmas favourite. Other works include *The Saint of Bleeker Street* (1954), *Maria Golovin* (1958) and *Le Dernier Sauvage*, first given in Paris in 1963. Now that opera is becoming less cut off from

music-theatre he is likely to thrive.

Ermanno Wolf-Ferrari (1876–1948) was half Italian, half German. His *I Gioelli della Madonna* (The Jewels of the Madonna, 1911) is *verismo*, his *I Quatro Rusteghi* (The Four Curmudgeons, 1906), known as *The School for Fathers* in Britain, is funny and charming. As for his *Il Segreto di Susanna* (1909), the secret is her smoking. *Il Campiello* (The Square, 1936) is often given in Italy; his first opera, *La Donna Curiose* (The Inquisitive Woman, 1903) in Germany.

Feruccio Busoni (1866–1924) was a great pianist as well as a composer. His double bill, *Turandot* and *Arlecchino*, was premiered in Dresden in 1925, but he died before finishing *Doktor Faust* (1925). Philipp Jarnach completed the score and the opera was much praised – by the few who heard it. Not until 1986 was its richness disclosed to large audiences, when the English National Opera presented it at the Coliseum in London.

Italian avant-garde composers include Dallapiccola, Luigi Nono and Fausto

The English National Opera's production of Busoni's Doctor Faust *was staged at the Coliseum in London in 1986, with Thomas Allen as Faust and Graham Clark as Mephistopheles. This was its first staged performance in Britain. It was produced by David Pountney and designed by Stefanos Lazaridis.*

Berio. Luigi Dallapiccola (1904–75), though using twelve-note technique, loved the voice, as his *Volo di Notte* (Night Flight, 1940) and the moving *Il Prigioniero* (The Prisoner, 1950) show. Luigi Nono (1924–) commented on the well-known evils in our society in *Intolleranza* (1960). Nino Rota (1911–) writes for films. His operas include the successful *Il Capello di Paglia di Firenze* (1955, based on the famous Italian farce, *The Italian Straw Hat*, while Federico Ghedini (1892–1965) had two major successes, *Billy Budd* (1949) and, his finest work, *Le Baccanti* (1948), which was premiered at La Scala. Yet can the old glory days return? Art marches on, but there are signs of marching backwards, not least with closer links with the musical theatre.

Adventurous audiences and some hundred opera houses are facts of life in the two Germanys, along with proper subsidies. Yet though no great composers have appeared since Richard Strauss to arouse mass feelings talent abounds, and some of it has made an impression in the wider world.

Hans Pfitzner (1869–1949) was a Wagnerian and Romantic nationalist whose *Palestrina* (1917) is well known in Germany. It is about a legendary event in the Italian composer's life and its 'angelic' scene is greatly admired.

Erich Korngold (1897–1957) had a great success with *Die Tote Stadt* (The Dead City, 1920) but he spent his later career composing rousing film scores for Warner Brothers.

Better known abroad than any of the above is the last genius of operetta, Franz Lehár (1870–1948). His masterpiece, *Die Lustige Witwe* (The Merry Widow, 1905) is better than many operas; his other works, *Giuditta*, *Der Graf von Luxembourg*, *Gipsy Love* and, above all *Das Land des Lächelns* (The Land of Smiles) being as delightful as they are truly musical joys. The great Mozartian tenor, Richard Tauber, helped Lehár's waning popularity in mid-career, though his temperamental behaviour sabotaged the run of *The Land of Smiles* at Drury Lane Theatre as he was so often absent.

Part of Lehár's strength lay in his own admiration of Puccini and Strauss, only the former responding to him. *The Merry Widow* is as perfect as *Fledermaus*. The

Gian Carlo Menotti's popular Amahl and the Night Visitors *(1951) was the first opera written for television. It was revived at Sadler's Wells Theatre in 1986 with the support of the Royal Opera House. James Rainbird was the twelve-year-old Amahl, with (left to right) Curtis Watson, John Dobson and Roderick Earle as the three kings.*

other major composers of operetta, Oscar Straus, Emmerich Kálmán and Leo Fall never reached his level.

When the *Widow* was first staged Arnold Schoenberg (1874–1951) was in his thirties. Four years later he wrote one of the first works that appeared to push tonality to its limits – in the year that Richard Strauss appeared to have done just that with *Elektra*. The opera in question was *Erwartung*. The composer's use of twelve-note music and his creation of 'speech-song' (*sprechgesang*) have made him greatly admired in the world of music, where his influence has been colossal. The ordinary opera-lover cannot be expected to get beyond respect, but since packed houses greeted Peter Hall's production of *Moses und Aron* at Covent Garden in 1965, drawn in, perhaps, by brilliant publicity and stories of debauchery on stage, the composer seems to be attracting the more adventurous members of the public for the right reasons.

Erwartung is a short, powerful monodrama. *Die glückliche Hand* (The Lucky Hand, 1913) outdoes Strindberg at his most nightmarish, while *Von Heute*

ABOVE
Schoenberg's unfinished masterpiece Moses und Aron *reached Covent Garden in 1965, having first been staged at Zurich in 1957. The British premiere was conducted by Solti and produced by Peter Hall, massive publicity ensuring full houses. Forbes Robinson and Richard Lewis played the title roles. Moses declaims in* sprechgesgang, *half speech, half song.*

RIGHT
English National Opera's production of The Merry Widow *in 1980 starred Anne Howells as a glittering Hanna Glavari, the widow of the title, pursued by Danilo, sung by Emile Belcourt. The exotic designs were by David Collis.*

auf Morgen (From One Day to the Next, 1930) is the first comic opera to use the twelve-note system (which the ordinary operagoer need not concern him or herself with). *Moses und Aron*, Schoenberg's masterpiece with its unfinished third act, was first staged in Zurich in 1957. This opera about communication between God and Man is a serious – and difficult – tragedy, its reputation is high and indeed many consider it great. By any standards it is powerful. The composer had a notable pupil, Alban Berg (1885–1935) who used Georg Büchner's drama *Wozzeck* to produce a modern masterpiece (1925).

This is a rare case of a modern opera creating a large following. It dates from 1925 and is *verismo* in that it is a 'slice of life', for the anti-hero is betrayed by his woman and kills her, after which he drowns himself. The score, once mastered, is passionate and moving, the construction brilliant, and the opera is showing signs of becoming truly popular. The unfinished *Lulu* was first staged in Zurich in 1937. It is based on two plays by Frank Wedekind, its heroine being a destructive *femme fatale*, finally murdered by Jack the Ripper. Widely admired by musicians, its growing number of appearances in the opera house have been major events, as at Covent Garden in 1981 with Karan Armstrong as Lulu, Götz Friedrich the producer, and Sir Colin Davis riding the whirlwind in the pit.

A brief mention must be made of Béla Bartók's one opera, *Duke Bluebeard's Castle* (1918), static but fascinating. More significant operatically is Paul Hindemith (1895–1963), whose *Cardillac* (1926) is about a goldsmith who kills to repossess his creations. *Neues vom Tage* (News of the Day), first seen in 1929, was revised in 1952. The Gas Company was not pleased by the opera as the heroine in her bath sang that she preferred electric heating. His masterpiece is *Mathis der Maler* (1938) about an actual painter, Matthias Grünewald. A peasant revolt on stage displeased the Nazi régime and got him exiled.

Ernst Křenek (1900–), born in Austria and moving to America in 1938, wrote his finest work before his move, the jazz opera, *Jonny spielt auf* (Johnny Strikes Up,

Alban Berg's Wozzeck *was revived at Covent Garden in 1984, with José van Dam as Wozzeck and Anja Silja as Marie. In the picture with her is the Drum Major (James King). The score, which sounded so difficult a generation ago to most operagoers, was brilliantly conducted by Christoph von Dohnányi.*

131

prising that Weill fled to America in 1935.

Weill's influence on opera was indirect, but by showing that there was a popular way to present modern opera, he performed a great service. So did his wife and finest interpreter, Lotte Lenya.

Carl Orff (1895–1982) is regularly abused for his *Carmina Burana* (1937), a cantata that is often staged and very easy on the ear. Medieval minstrel songs about love, life and nature with percussive effects entertain or infuriate depending on the listener. Other works include the tuneful *Der Mond* (The Moon, 1939).

Berg's Lulu *at last reached Covent Garden in 1983 in the striking shape of Karan Armstrong, the star of a highly theatrical production by Götz Friedrich, designed by Timothy O'Brien, with Colin Davis conducting. Karan Armstrong's performance, in one of the most challenging of roles, was a triumph.*

1927). It is about a black who steals a violin and conquers the world with his dance music. A success in continental Europe, it was cold-shouldered by Americans, who might be expected to know what jazz was all about.

Outside Germany Kurt Weill (1900–50) is much better known, not least because of his partnership with Bertholt Brecht. Their first joint work was the masterpiece inspired by *The Beggar's Opera*, *Die Dreigroschenoper* (The Three-penny Opera, 1928), Weill's sourly romantic popular style being much admired. Far finer was *The Rise and Fall of the City of Mahagonny* (1930), a satire about an American town obsessed with material pleasures. This was a brilliant and enjoyable political opera, as was *Die Bürghschaft* (Hostage) in 1932 to Caspar Neher's libretto, and it was hardly sur-

Catulli Carmina (1943) is based on the life and work of the Roman poet Catullus and with *Trionfi dell'Afrodite* (1953) and *Carmina Burana* it became a triple bill called *Trionfi*. *Die Kluge* (The Clever Woman 1943), is generally considered to be his best work for the stage.

The much younger Hans Werner Henze (1926–   ) has been fairly treated by English opera houses. His treatment of the Manon story, *Boulevard Solitude* (1952) made his name and was followed by a radio opera, *Das Ende einer Welt* (The End of the World, 1953). A disciple of Schoenberg, but biased in favour of lyricism, he is fascinated by the artist's relation to himself and to society. A stay in Italy resulted in even more exotic lyrical writing, and his operas *Das König Hirsch* (The King Stag, 1956), *Der Prinz von Homburg* (1960) and *Elegy for Young Lovers* (1961) with a text by W.H. Auden and Chester Kallman, increased his reputation. This last was produced at Glyndebourne and is about the artist and his relation to society, and how he devours his friends to improve his art. The same writers adapted Euripides' *The*

The National Theatre's production of Brecht's The Threepenny Opera *in 1986, with Tim Curry in the role of Macheath. Brecht and the composer Kurt Weill brought the action forward two centuries from the time when the work that inspired it,* The Beggar's Opera, *was set.*

Bacchae which became *The Bassarids* (1966), a magical and powerful score, and Henze was invited to both produce and conduct it by the English National Opera in 1974. It was given a respectful hearing but did not stay in the repertory. *We Came to the River* failed at its Covent Garden premiere in 1976.

Manuel de Falla (1876–1946) has been Spain's most notable composer from the moment his nationalist and impressionist *La Vide Breve* (A Short Life, 1905, produced 1913) was staged. It is a heady blend of strong drama and Spanish popular life, its tragic heroine Salud being a major creation. Other operas of his include *El Retablo de Maese Pedro* (1923), from an episode in *Don Quixote* and *Atlantida* (1961) posthumously produced after being completed by Ernst Halffter. Enrique Granados (1867–1916) composed *zarzuelas*, also one major opera, *Goyescas*, which was premiered at the Metropolitan, New York in 1916. Returning, his ship was torpedoed and he lost his life trying to save his wife.

After *Pelléas et Melisande*, another great impressionist, Maurice Ravel, wrote two short operas, both more theatrical than Debussy's. *L'Heure Espagnole* (The Spanish Hour, 1911) is an entertainingly bawdy one-acter, while *L'Enfant et les Sortilèges* (The Child and the Enchantments, 1925) with a text by Colette, is a little gem about a naughty boy who gets his come-uppance from furniture, books and toys in the first

Hans Werner Henze's The Bassarids *(1966) was staged by English National Opera in 1974, produced by the composer with designs by Timothy O'Brien and Tazeena Firth. The opera is inspired by the Greek play,* The Bacchae *of Euripides. In a splendid, committed cast, Katherine Pring was outstanding, and there were fine performances by Josephine Barstow, Norman Welsby and Tom McDonnell.*

part of the opera and trees and animals in the second part!

Meanwhile, Offenbach's influence made for a stream of operettas including Lecocq's *La Fille de Madame Angot* (1872), Robert Planquette's *Les Cloches de Corneville* (1877) and by André Messager – who conducted the first *Pelléas* – *Veronique*, *Monsieur Beaucaire* (1919) and other delightful concoctions. Despite the great Lehár, however, operetta faded into musical comedy which, however entertaining, is not a subject for this book.

On the serious front Arthur Honegger (1892–1955) triumphed with *Le Roi David* (1921). Conceived as an opera, it appeared, however, as an oratorio. He wrote *Judith* (1926) and *Antigone* (1927) but his best

known work is *Jeanne d'Arc au Bûcher* (at the stake) in 1936. Part opera, part oratorio, with Joan as a speaking role, the whole combines into a major work. Paul Claudel's text is very fine. With Ibert he later wrote *L'Aiglon* (The Eagle) from Rostand's play about Napoleon's son.

Darius Milhaud (1892–1974) collaborated with Jean Cocteau in *Le Pauvre Matelot* (1927) a grim melodrama economically put across in contrast to his huge *Christophe Colomb* (1930) to a text by Claudel, and with film included. *Bolivar* (1943) was less notable, but *David* (1950) was a huge conception for Jerusalem's 3,000th birthday and triumphed at La Scala and elsewhere.

Francis Poulenc (1899–1963) wrote two

Ravel's delightful L'Enfant et les Sortilèges (The Child and the Enchantments) was staged at Covent Garden in 1983 with designs by David Hockney which were first seen at New York's Metropolitan Opera in 1981. The book of the opera is by Colette. Ann Murray was the child.

135

comedies, *Le Gendarme Incompris* (1920) and the scintillating *Les Mamelles de Tirésias* (1944) in which a husband changes sexes. In contrast *Dialogues des Carmélites* (1957) is a sombrely impressive religious work set in the Revolution, which has a shattering final scene as the nuns go to their deaths at the guillotine. Poulenc also wrote a forty-five minute monodrama to a text by Cocteau, *La Voix Humaine*, a jilted lover speaking over the telephone to the man who has left her. Poulenc composed it for Denise Duval.

There have been three notable Swiss composers. Rolf Libermann (1910–), Heinrich Sutermeister (1910–) and Frank Martin (1890–1974). Libermann

ABOVE
Francis Poulenc's Dialogues Des Carmélites (The Carmelites) *was successfully revived at Covent Garden in 1983, sung in English, with Régine Crespin as Mme de Croissy, Felicity Lott as Blanche, Lillian Watson as Sister Constance and Valerie Masterson as Mme Lidoin. The last scene at the guillotine was, as always, one of the most shattering in all opera.*

RIGHT
English National Opera staged Prokofiev's The Gambler *in 1983, produced by David Pountney, designed by Maria Bjørnson and conducted by Christian Bades. The production was first staged at the Netherlands Opera in 1975. Seen here is the gambling scene. Graham Clark (centre) gave a striking performance as Alexei, the gambler, and other notable performances were given by Sally Burgess, Jean Rigby, Ann Howard and John Tomlinson.*

who was in charge of the Hamburg Opéra from 1959, took over the Paris Opéra (1973–80) and made it into a great house once again. His operas include *Leonore 40/ 45* (1952) about a German soldier and a French girl in the Second World War, *Penelope* (1954) and *The School for Wives* (1955). His use of parody, jazz and twelve-note music add to his gift for striking effects.

Heinrich Sutermeister, a pupil of Orff, is best known for his *Romeo und Julia* (1940), which was produced at Sadler's Wells in 1952, and his other operas include *Raskolnikov*, a version of *Crime and Punishment*. Frank Martin, well known for his opera-oratorio on the Tristan story, *Le Vin Herbé* (The Love

Potion, 1941) only wrote one true opera, *Der Sturm* (1956), based on Shakespeare's *The Tempest*.

The great Igor Stravinsky (1882–1971) wrote two operas, the early *Le Rossignol* (The Nightingale, 1914) being a lush spectacular piece. His next theatrical works are hard to define for *Les Noces* (1914–17) is more ballet than opera, while *Renard* (1922) confines singers to the orchestra pit. *Mavra* (1922) is a one-act *opera buffa* and a counterblast to Wagner. There followed an opera-oratorio with a text by Cocteau after Sophocles, *Oedipus Rex* (1927) with a speaker providing the narrative. The music blazes. At last came a full opera, *The Rake's Progress* (1951) with a libretto by W.H. Auden and Chester Kallman, following the famous Hogarth engravings. The music is neo-Mozartian, the opera is masterly.

Censorship has badly handicapped Russian opera, the Party considering that anything in advance of Tchaikovsky was taboo at one grim period in the 1940s. This meant trouble for two geniuses, Serge Prokofiev (1891–1953) and Dmitri Shostakovich (1906–75). The former, a pupil of Rimsky-Korsakov, sensibly became popular but was denounced all the same. His first surviving opera, *The Gambler*, was held up by the Revolution and finally staged in Brussels in 1929. Its brilliance was at once recognized and the very different *The Love for Three Oranges*, staged in Chicago in 1921, confirmed his promise, the opera being an amazing

Stravinsky's The Rake's Progress was staged at Glyndebourne in 1975 with striking settings by David Hockney, the opera being produced by John Cox. Bernard Haitink conducted. Jill Gomez (seated) was Ann Truelove, Leo Goeke, Tom Rakewell, and Rosalind Elias, Baba the Turk.

137

romantic fantasy based on a comedy by Carlo Gozzi. It is very entertaining, if heartless.

The Fiery Angel, finally staged at Venice in 1955, is about possession and sorcery and is superb music-theatre, the role of Renata being a great one. Other operas followed but in 1948 he was criticized by the philistine Zhdanov Tribunal, the object of their displeasure being *The Story of a Real Man* (1948).

There followed *War and Peace* (1941–42). The composer kept revising it until his death. After concert performances it was staged at Florence in 1953 and Leningrad in 1955. The opera assumes a knowledge of Tolstoy, but that said, it must be stressed that it is a glorious work. 'Peace' is finer than 'War' but despite the cutting of the enormous story it remains a classic example of a modern popular opera. Many consider it a masterpiece.

Shostakovich's Lady Macbeth of Mtsensk *(also known as* Katerina Ismailova) *was a great success in Russia until it was suddenly banned (probably by Stalin) in 1936 – for thirty years. It is a most powerful work. This is the production by the State Opera of South Australia, with Beverley Bergen singing the title role. John Tasker directed and Patrick Thomas conducted.*

Shostakovich ran into even more trouble. *The Nose* (1930), from a Gogol story, upset Authority because it was musically eccentric, while his masterpiece, *Lady Macbeth of Mtsensk* (1934), from the story by Nikolai Leskov, first acclaimed as a model of Soviet realism, was later savaged by *Pravda*. Revised, it returned as *Katerina Ismailova*, the name of the murderous wife who is memorably and sympathetically drawn.

Other Soviet composers stayed within the system, a fine example being the historical *The Decembrists* by Yuri Shaporin, completed in 1953, about a stirring incident in Tsarist history. It is as easy on the ear as Tchaikovsky and it

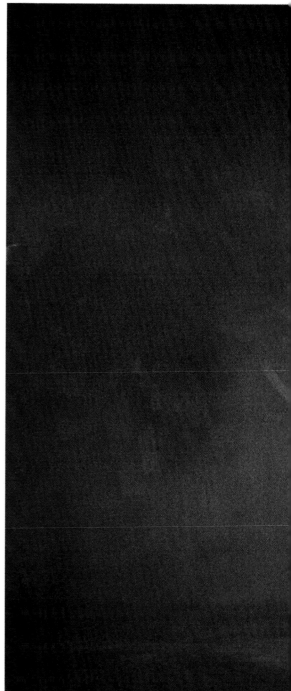

works, while many uncensored modern operas do not.

In the last decade, and to the joy of his longtime admirers, Leoš Janáček (1854–1928) has become very popular. (The author of this book can remember nights at Sadler's Wells where the audience cannot have reached 200. But it is to the Sadler's Wells Opera that lovers of his music owe their thanks.) Fears of his unusual plots, his allegedly difficult or-

chestration, have vanished since the first production of *Katya Kabanova* at the Wells in 1951. He has conquered British audiences at last. Now the only problem is whether his audiences should be helped by surtitles.

He made his name with his most instantly appealing opera, *Jenufa* (1904). Its lyricism makes it an ideal start to the discovery of the composer, also its suggestion of folk-tunes which are not in fact used. Jenufa, and her foster-mother who murders her daughter's illegitimate child are great creations. The best known of his operas are *Katya Kabanova* (1921) after the Russian Ostrovsky's *The Storm*, *The Cunning Little Vixen* (1924), a glorious hymn to nature, *The Makropoulos Case* (1926) from Capek's play about the 300-year-old woman who remains a beauty, and *From the House of the Dead* (1930) from Dostoevsky's novel of his own experiences in a Siberian labour camp, a powerful, indeed shattering, work. Other

Prokofiev's masterpiece, War and Peace, was revived by English National Opera in 1984, the performance – on a vast scale – showing the company's ensemble to tremendous advantage. Seen here is Malcolm Donnelly as Napoleon.

139

RIGHT
In 1969 Peter Pears once again sang the part of the Male chorus in Britten's The Rape of Lucretia, *a role that he had created in 1946. The 1969 performance by the English National Opera Group had Janet Baker as Lucretia and Heather Harper as the Female Chorus, and the fine cast included John Shirley Quirk and Benjamin Luxon.*

OPPOSITE TOP
The premiere of Yuri Lyubimov's production of Janáček's Jenufa *at Covent Garden in 1986 was a thrilling occasion. Bernard Haitink conducted and as the Kostelnićka, Eva Randova enjoyed a personal triumph. Ashley Putnam, Philip Langridge and Neil Rosenshein contributed fine performances, and surtitles made their Royal Opera House debut, welcomed – it would seem – by most operagoers.*

OPPOSITE BOTTOM
Janáček's Katya Kabanova *was produced by Günter Krämer for Deutsche Oper, Berlin in March 1986. Karan Armstrong sang the title role with Stephen Algie as Boris Grigoryevich. The conductor was Jiri Kout.*

operas include *Osud* (Fate), now known to British audiences. Even his two-part opera, *Mr Brouček's Excursion to the Moon* and *Mr Brouček's Excursion to the Fifteenth Century* are no longer *terra incognita*. He is now rightly regarded as one of our century's masters.

Benjamin Britten's *Peter Grimes* (1945) is one of the most astonishing first operas in history. (Purists may recall *Paul Bunyan*, staged at Columbia University in 1941, but this was an operetta, not a real opera.) Before discussing *Grimes* it must be noted that it did not create English (or British) opera overnight. There had indeed been some modest foreign excursions for English works. Yet Balfe and his contemporaries were pale copies of Italian composers, understandably enough. The Irishman Sir Charles Stanford (1852–1924) tried to establish English opera especially with *Shamus O'Brien* (1896) and *The Travelling Companion* (1925), the second being given at Sadler's Wells where Lilian Baylis (1874–1937) reigned from 1931 as she had reigned at the Old Vic from 1914. She was a God-intoxicated, inspired, earthy, invincible, self-educated, glorious woman who, without subsidy but with much prayer, created the Old Vic Theatre Company (now the National Theatre), Sadler's Wells Opera, previously at the Old Vic, and now the English National Opera, and what is now the Royal Ballet (assisted, of course, by Ninette de Valois). Yet before her day the English musical renaissance, exemplified by Elgar, only produced minor works.

The redoubtable Dame Ethel Smyth (1858–1944) wrote six operas, the best being *The Wreckers* (1906) and *The Boatswain's Mate* (1916) which show her German training. Sir Thomas Beecham, who spent a fortune on presenting well-performed opera, championed her and even more ardently championed Frederick Delius, Yorkshire-born of German Scandinavian descent. He trained in Leipzig, and later lived in France, also having a spell growing oranges in Florida. His best known opera is *A Village Romeo and Juliet* (1901, produced 1907). First staged in Berlin, Beecham presented it at Covent Garden in 1910, its interlude, 'The Walk to the Paradise Garden' becoming very popular. Despite Beecham's efforts,

141

Delius's *Irmelin*, *Koanga* and *Fennimore and Gerda* never caught on but Beecham gave seasons of opera in London and Manchester that became legendary and lost him a fortune in the process.

Gustav Holst (1874–1934) tried to succeed in opera; *The Perfect Fool* (1923) has some good operatic parodies, and his *Savitri* (1916) was admired, yet, like the very English Ralph Vaughan Williams (1872–1958), he never achieved real success. However Vaughan Williams achieved one fine ballad opera, strangely neglected now, *Hugh the Drover* (1924) set in Napoleonic times. His finest work is possibly the one-act *Riders to the Sea* (1937) with text by J.M. Synge.

Rutland Boughton (1878–1960) seemed destined to fame after *The Immortal Hour* (1922) and he hoped to make Glastonbury an English Bayreuth. He did not succeed. Yet opera itself was gaining ground

ABOVE
Benjamin Britten's Billy Budd *was first staged at Covent Garden in 1951. Some recognized its greatness at once, many more have discovered it since – indeed its second half is opera at its most powerful and sublime. In this Covent Garden production of 1964 Robert Kerns is Billy, Forbes Robinson is Claggart and at the table are Ronald Lewis, Robert Savoie and David Kelly.*

RIGHT
Jon Vickers and Heather Harper at Covent Garden in Britten's first masterpiece, Peter Grimes. *This outstanding occasion happily survives on video.*

thanks to Lilian Baylis' beloved, if un-fashionable, Sadler's Wells Opera. What Britain needed was a master and a master-piece and it got both.

In the Second World War Covent Garden had been turned into a dance hall, showing the tenuous hold that opera had at the time. But Sadler's Wells Opera, its theatre bombed in the war, was touring and preparing one of the greatest surprises in operatic history, a native masterpiece, *Peter Grimes* (1945) by Benjamin Britten.

Britten (1913–76) was by far the most successful operatic composer in British history and he has a wide public who love his operas as other great masters are loved, and widely admired overseas. His first opera presents a softened version of the Grimes in George Crabbe's poem, *The Borough*; Montague Slater providing the libretto. Its hero is the first of Britten's outsiders. Characterization is masterly throughout, while the sea off Britten's beloved Suffolk coast permeates the score. Grimes is misunderstood by ordi-nary kindly people and even alienates his one true friend, Ellen Orford, whose 'Let her among you without fault' is just one superb lyrical outburst. Grimes has ex-traordinary moments including the haunting 'Now the Great Bear and Ple-iades,' while the townspeople are super-bly characterized as they range from kindness and jollity to hatred. The Moon-light Prelude before Act III is simple, beautiful and shattering – and leads straight into an entertaining scene with a dance in the background. We are in Britten's beloved Aldeburgh around 1830 and in the presence of operatic genius. This opera transformed the operatic scene as John Osborne's *Look Back In Anger* transformed the British theatre eleven years later.

The English National Opera's revival of Benjamin Britten's Gloriana *at the Coliseum in 1984 had Sarah Walker as Elizabeth I and Anthony Rolfe-Johnson as the Earl of Essex (left). On the right is Neil Howlett as Mountjoy.*

Britten founded the English Opera Group in 1946 with John Piper and Eric Crozier to create new operas and encourage poets and playwrights to write librettos. *The Rape of Lucretia* (1946) with a 12-piece orchestra was the first, striking result, then Eric Crozier transferred a Maupassant story to Suffolk and the result was the enchanting and hilarious *Albert Herring* (1947). Britten now did a version of the *The Beggar's Opera* (1948) and the next year gave young and old *Let's Make an Opera*, the participants making and performing *The Little Sweep*. Britten provided his realization of Purcell's *Dido and Aeneas* in 1951, which also saw another superb work, *Billy Budd*, from the Melville story. Set on a man-of war in Napoleonic times, the first act is very fine, the second deeply moving and sheer genius, only the evil Claggart not being totally convincing. For many this is Britten's masterpiece. *Gloriana*, written for the Coronation in 1953, survived a gala opening with an understandably unsuitable audience, to become yet another favourite, though, Queen Elizabeth I and Essex apart, characterization is less deep than usual in Britten's work. *The Turn of the Screw* (1954) from a Henry James story is a chamber opera of great flair and quality, which can survive in the huge Coliseum, where it was directed by Jonathan Miller. *Noyes Fludde* (1958) from one of the Chester cycle of mystery plays is surely the finest work for children since *Hänsel und Gretel*, while *A Midsummer's Night's Dream* (1960) whether as chamber opera or at Covent Garden is as successful as it is delightful, though the lovers' music is not quite as inspired as the fairy music and that for the marvellous Mechanicals. The Pyramus and Thisbe scene is a triumph, a Donizettian pastiche complete with a mad scene à la *Lucia*, while the opera ends with the sublime use of children's voices. Oberon is a counter-tenor role and Puck is spoken and played by a boy. That ardent music-lover Shakespeare would have approved.

Three Parables for Church Performance followed between 1964 and 1968, *Curlew River*, *The Burning Fiery Furnace* and *The Prodigal Son*, then came *Owen Wingrave*. Taken from a Henry James story, this was below Britten's standard because he loaded the dice so heavily

145

against the military family, who object to the hero's pacifism, that they become mere one-dimensional characters, thus weakening the work artistically – music-ally as well as dramatically. Happily, the last opera, *Death in Venice* (1973), saw the composer reach greatness again, the score being dazzlingly inventive, the story grip-ping. Peter Pears excelled himself in the great leading role.

Thus ended an operatic career which was not only a great one, but proved the viability of modern opera so triumphant-ly. Sir William Walton (1902–83) wrote only two operas, *Troilus and Cressida* (1954) with a libretto based on Chaucer and some true romantic music, and *The*

Bear (1967) from a Chekhov farce. Sir Michael Tippett (1905–   ) has achieved a large following now on both sides of the Atlantic, which has resulted in new enthu-siasm for his operas. These include *The Midsummer Marriage* (1955), a ravishing score, *King Priam* (1962) sparser and dramatic, *The Knot Garden* (1970) and *The Ice Break* (1977). *The Knot Garden*'s score is greatly admired, though the habit of writing his own librettos has not been enthusiastically welcomed by some of his admirers. The wide-ranging tenor Robert Tear has been notably successful in Tippett's works.

The Australian Malcolm Williamson had some successes in the 1960s, his first

Harrison Birtwhistle's Punch and Judy *was first performed in 1968 at the Aldeburgh Festival, with Maureen Morelle as Judy and John Cameron as Punch. David Atherton conducted, and the production was by Anthony Besch. Peter Rice was the designer.*

opera being *Our Man in Havana*. He was before his time. He dared to write tunes and was damned for it. Thus works like *The Violins of St. Jacques* and *The English Eccentrics* were over-strongly attacked.

More and more composers are working in opera. One of the most prolific is Harrison Birtwhistle (1934–), whose works include *Punch and Judy*, *Down by the Greenwood Side*, *Bowdown*, *The Mask of Orpheus*, and *Yan Tan Tethera*, a 'Mechanical Pastoral' with a text by Tony Harrison. Oliver Knussen has achieved appealing children's operas with *Where the Wild Things Are* and *Higglety Pigglety Pop*; Nichols Maw's romantic opera *The Rising of the Moon* was staged at Glyndebourne in 1970; Thea Musgrave's operas include *Mary, Queen of Scots, A Christmas Carol* and *Harriet, the Woman Called Moses* (1985) about Harriet Tubman, the black heroine who led many slaves to freedom in the North.

Richard Rodney Bennett has written a number of operas including *Penny for a Song* (1967). Alexander Goehr's *Arden Must Die* made a powerful impression at its German premiere in 1967, but he is now more concerned with music theatre. The public in Britain remains conservative when faced with new music, but less so than formerly. Britten's popularity remains unique for a native opera composer.

Michael Tippett's The Knot Garden *was first staged in 1970 before the surge of interest in his music had got under way. Produced by Peter Hall and designed by Timothy O'Brien, the cast included (left to right) Robert Tear, Thomas Hemsley, Jill Gomez, Josephine Barstow and Yvonne Minton.*

Harriet Tubman was a heroic black slave who escaped to freedom before the Civil War, and then returned to lead some 300 others to freedom. Thea Musgrave used this splendid story for her Harriet, The Woman Called Moses *(1985) which was staged by Virginia Opera Association in Norfolk, Virginia with great success. Cynthia Haymon was Harriet.*

America is better known for a long succession of fine singers than for its native composers, who have existed since soon after the Revolution. The conservative Metropolitan Opera welcomed Deems Taylor's *Peter Ibbetson* in 1931. In 1935 came George Gershwin's *Porgy and Bess*, which has now been staged at Glyndebourne (1986). The work is established as *the* American national opera and no one would now doubt that it is a masterpiece. Samuel Barber's *Vanessa* (1958) and *Antony and Cleopatra* (1966) have been respected rather than loved, while in the 1930s Virgil Thomson's *Four Saints in Three Flats* made a brief impression. Aaron Copland (1900–) is best known for his ballet scores rather than opera, but *The Tender Land*, set in the

Depression, is a hauntingly evocative work.

Marc Blizstein (1905–1964) is best known for *The Cradle Will Rock* (1937): produced by Orson Welles, it was a fiery anti-capitalist piece and disliked by Authority. His version of *The Threepenny Opera* (1954) ran for 2250 performances. Philip Glass (1937–) made a striking impression with *Einstein on the Beach*. *Satyagraha*, which concerns the life and career of Ghandi, premiered in Rotterdam in 1980. *Akhnaten*, premiered in Stuttgart in 1984, has achieved a huge international success with the haunting rhythmic patterns of Glass's highly individual music.

There is tremendous operatic activity in the United States today, and barriers between opera and Broadway – and London's West End – are crumbling. Who would dare say that Bernstein's fabulous *Candide* is not operatic? *Sweeney Todd* is operatic also, while so to a lesser degree is *The Phantom of the Opera* by Lloyd Webber. *West Side Story* (1957) embraced all the theatre arts though, alas, Leonard Bernstein has only written one opera, *Trouble in Tahiti*. For a musical to aspire to opera the music must be good. But opera as a word can range widely. *The Phantom of the Opera* is more viable as opera than too many over-modern scores. The current cross-fertilization is good for all. Better still would be a worthy successor to Mozart, Wagner and Verdi – and Puccini, Strauss and Gershwin.

George Gershwin's Porgy and Bess *was a colossal success at the 1986 Glyndebourne Festival, produced by Trevor Nunn and designed by John Napier. The conductor was Simon Rattle. The leading roles were brilliantly performed by Willard White and Cynthia Haymon. At the end the audience stood and cheered, a Glyndebourne 'first'.*

Opera: some definitions and descriptions

Aria
The elaborate song-form of opera and oratorio, from the Italian for 'air'.

Arietta
A shorter, simpler aria.

Arioso
An aria-like vocal form, roughly half way between an aria and recitative.

Baritone
The male voice between tenor and bass.

Bass
The deepest male voice. Several countries have sub-divisions of this and other voices.

Bass-baritone
Not, as might be supposed, simply a voice between bass and baritone, but the voice required for certain parts – Wotan, Hans Sachs, Boris, etc. – demanding lyricism and the depths of a *basso profondo*.

Bel canto
A rather imprecise term meaning beautiful singing or beautiful song. *Bel canto* flourished in Italy from the 17th to 19th centuries, with the stress on lovely tone, perfect technique and smooth phrasing. Drama was less in evidence than in the German style, yet the most admired artists of the early 19th century who used the Italian style, Pasta and Malibran, were intensely dramatic, as was Callas when she did so much in the 1950s to revive the art of *bel canto*. And a major Verdian role without dramatic singing as well as beautiful tone is a negation of what the composer intended.

Brindisi
A drinking song, from the Italian 'far brindisi,' meaning 'to drink one's health'.

Buffo
A singer of comic roles, as in 'basso buffo'. From the Italian for 'gust' or 'puff'.

Cabaletta
Though this can mean a short simple aria with repeats, as used by Rossini and others, or a recurring passage in an aria, the opera-goer is most likely to meet it as the brilliant, usually swift, last section of an aria. Verdi raised the form to fiery, often electrifying, heights.

Cadenza
A virtuoso display by a singer (or instrumentalist) at the end of an aria, notably in 18th-century music. It could be dragged out far beyond legitimate ornamentation, as indeed some pianists do to this day.

Cantilena
Vocal writing that is smooth and tuneful, or an indication by a composer that such singing is required.

Canzone
A song in an opera that is not part of the action, a famous example being the Veil Song in *Don Carlo*, sung by Eboli.

Castrato
Though this sad subject is dealt with in Chapter 1, it may be amplified a little. Castrati entered opera because there was a shortage of trained women singers, while some countries banned females on stage (as did England until the Restoration). Long after opera abandoned them – though as late as the 1820s Meyerbeer wrote a role for Velluti, the last great castrato, in *Il Crociato in Egitto* – the Vatican continued using male sopranos and altos, castrated before puberty.

Cavatina
A short aria.

Claque
Hired applauders, who strangely do more good than harm, whatever the essential fraudulence of their 'profession'. Many are students and indigent music-lovers and they merely get free tickets, as opposed to their leader who is paid. A good leader can transform a dull audience in Italy, Vienna, etc, by carefully-timed expressions of joy – as opposed to anti-claques who are basically hired assassins out to wreck, as has happened to Callas and others in our own times. The most notable example of the artistic integrity of a claque occurred at Parma, that rugged hot-bed of passionate enthusiasm, where once the local claque returned a tenor's fee to him and proceeded to boo his every performance until he fled the town.

Coloratura
Elaborate ornament of a melody, from the German 'Koloratur', hence the *coloratura* soprano.

Comprimario
The small part artist in opera. Both Barbarina in *Figaro* and Spoletta in *Tosca* are *comprimario* roles, though the former is often a stepping-stone to larger roles, whereas the *comprimario* singer is normally a specialist in such parts.

Contralto
The lowest woman's voice.

Continuo
A part played throughout a work in the bass line, on the harpsichord, organ, etc.

Contrapuntal
It is the adjective of counterpoint, which is the method of combining two or more melodies simultaneously, yet making musical sense out of them.

Counter-tenor
A voice higher than a tenor's using an exceptional amount of head resonance. It is not a falsetto voice and is not to be confused with a castrato. The most notable part written for it is Oberon in Britten's *A Midsummer Night's Dream*. Few counter-tenors have enough power for a large opera house, one exception being James Bowman.

Da Capo aria
An aria in three sections, the third being a repeat of the first. In use from c. 1650–1790.

Dramma Giocoso

Mozart so described *Don Giovanni*. The term was used mainly in the 18th century to describe a comic opera with serious or tragic scenes.

Dramma per musica

A term used in the 17th and 18th centuries to describe a libretto and its serious operatic treatment.

Festivals

The oldest European opera festival is Bayreuth's, which began in 1876 with the first complete *Ring*. Many so-called festivals, however enjoyable, are really a glamorous part of the ordinary opera season, but the truest festivals have an identity of their own. Among them are Salzburg, which has been famous since its start in the 1920s, not simply for its Mozart, but for Strauss, Verdi, etc, and many modern works. A new Festspielhaus was built in 1960, which houses the Easter Festival, the creation of von Karajan, whose Wagnerian performances during it are famous. Perhaps the most legendary performances were given under Toscanini from 1935 to 1937, including *Falstaff*, *Fidelio*, *Zauberflöte* and *Meistersinger*. The greatest open air festival is in the Verona Arena, greatest in locale, size of audiences and performance standards. Other notable festivals include Glyndebourne (1934), Edinburgh (1947), Spoleto (1958), Florence (1933), Santa Fé (1957), Aix-en-Provence (1948), Aldeburgh (1948), and Wexford (1951). Some have superstars, others stars in the making, some are tourist attractions. The performances at Bregenz's festival (1946) are held on a 'floating stage' on the shores of Lake Constance.

Fioritura

The decoration added to a melody, either with written or improvised figures, the word being the Italian for flowering. From the 17th to the early 19th centuries adding *fioriture* was traditional practice, though sometimes it was so abused by singers that composers could not recognize their own music. Yet when a great or good artist added such ornaments, the result enhanced the music. Soprano Joan Sutherland in roles like *Lucia di Lammermoor* has discreetly and bril-

liantly revived the old skill, but it can come as a shock to a modern audience in, say, *Figaro*, to hear ornaments in the second verse of 'Voi che sapete', however historically correct. Even an *appogiatura*, where the main note is delayed by a grace-note, can be startling to those not used to hearing them in a Mozart aria, for example.

Grand opera

In Anglo-American countries, another word for opera, though officially it means serious opera without spoken dialogue. However, in France grand opera means a large-scale work, with chorus and ballet, in four or five acts, as exemplified in the operas of Meyerbeer.

Intermezzo

The more usual use of the word means a short piece between scenes, as in *Cavalleria Rusticana*; in other words, it is an interlude, either of original music, or developing themes that have already been heard, as in *Manon Lescaut*.

Leitmotiv

Meaning 'leading motive' in German, it is a short musical phrase which characterizes a person, idea or thing. Wagner was its chief and most brilliant exponent.

Maestro

The Italian's descriptive name for composers and conductors. In Germany the conductor is called a Kapellmeister, though this once meant the choir-master of a Court chapel. The Italian equivalent was *maestro di capella*.

Mezza voce

Singing at half power, from the Italian for half-voice.

Mezzo-soprano

The middle female voice.

Opera buffa

The term for 18th-century Italian comic opera, as opposed to *opera seria* (see below).

Opéra comique

Though this signifies comic opera in French, it has two meanings. The first refers to 18th-century French comic

operas with spoken dialogue, the second to 19th-century French operas with spoken dialogue, comic or not. So serious operas like *Carmen* and *Lakmé* rank as *opéra comique*.

Opera seria

Though the term simply means 'serious' opera, it normally refers to the Italian operas of the 18th century with their mythological or heroic plots, formal music and (lack of) drama, sometimes tortuous librettos and regular use of *castrati* singers (see above). Mozart's *Idomeneo* (1781) is proof that the stultifying form could occasionally be transcended. Technically superb singers of great influence allowed it to survive so long, as did their audience. Rossini's *Semiramide* (1823) is a late example.

Parlando

The singer, directed by the composer, lets the voice sound approximately like speech. A famous example occurs in Act 2 of *Tosca* when the heroine has killed Scarpia and rejoices in amazement: 'E avanti a lui tremeva tutta Roma!' – 'And all Rome trembled before him!'.

Prima donna

'First Lady'. The leading female singer in an opera, or the star soprano of a company.

Répétiteur

His job is to coach the singers in their roles and he may conduct off-stage bands, etc. in performance. Many conductors have started in this post, which is called *solo répétiteur* in Germany and *maestro collaboratore* in Italy.

Scena

A dramatic solo less formal than an aria, often less lyrical, a supreme example being Leonore's 'Abscheulicher' in *Fidelio*.

Singspiel

A German form of English ballad opera and French *opéra comique*, which developed in the 18th century.

Soubrette

The word means 'cunning' in French and operatically refers to clever servant girls like Despina and Susanna, though it may also mean a light soprano comedienne role like Adèle in *Fledermaus*.

Soprano
The highest female voice. There are too many sub-divisions to list here, but two words which often appear in reviews may be noted. Desdemona in *Otello* is a *soprano lirico spinto* role, and 'spinto' means urged or pushed on, while Norina in *Don Pasquale* is a *soprano leggiero*, the latter word meaning 'light' or 'lightly'.

Sprechgesang
'Speech-song', originated by Schoenberg and used by Berg, in which the singer emits, but does not sustain, the note. It is a blend of speech and song, but is not the same as *parlando* (see above).

Stagione
The Italian word for season, but in its widest sense it has an important meaning. A *stagione* opera house like La Scala, or Covent Garden since the early 1950s, gives a limited number of performances of certain operas, some of them new productions, and all with as few cast changes as possible.

These productions may or may not be revived later. This raises standards considerably even if not so many operas are on display as there are in a repertory house like the Vienna State Opera. A vast number of productions may be seen in such a house, with many cast changes, and the result is that, except at festival times, standards are overall lower than at a *stagione* house. Artistically, *stagione* must rank as the finer system.

Tenor
The highest male voice (but see Counter-tenor). Most of the variations explain themselves, such as the vivid *tenore di forza*, which admirably describes the role of Otello.

Tessitura
The average range of an aria in relation to the voice for which it has been written. Turandot's 'In questa reggia' for instance has a notoriously high tessitura. The term can also be used of a singer's voice.

Transposition
Some singers transpose an aria down to be able to cope better with high notes, though only those with perfect pitch can be sure of catching them out if the transposition is minimal. A singer can transpose up as well.

Travesti
Breeches-roles in opera such as Cherubino in *Figaro*, Octavian in *Rosenkavalier*, etc., the male characters being taken by women.

Twelve-note music
Music based on all the twelve (black and white) notes of the scale as opposed to the seven notes of the diatonic scale. (*Note:* there is no simple way of describing the above.)

Verismo
Meaning 'realism' in Italian, it is used to describe the realistic school that began with Mascagni's *Cavalleria Rusticana* (1890).

Zarzuela
A popular style of Spanish ballad opera, usually in one act. It has been popular for several centuries and deals with, and sometimes satirizes, subjects close to the people. Improvisation and audience participation are features of the genre, along with easily enjoyable music.

The world's repertoire: a selection of composers and their works

Albert, Eugene d'Albert (1864–1932)
 Tiefland (1903)
Bartók, Béla (1881–1945)
 Duke Bluebeard's Castle (1911, produced 1918)
Beethoven, Ludwig van (1770–1827)
 Fidelio (1805/1806/1814)
Bellini, Vincenzo (1801–35)
 Il Pirata (1827), *I Capuleti e i Montecchi* (1830), *La Sonnambula* (1831), *Norma* (1831), *Beatrice di Tenda* (1833), *I Puritani* (1835)
Berg, Alban (1885–1935)
 Wozzeck (1925), *Lulu* (unfinished, produced 1937)
Berlioz, Hector (1803–69)
 Benvenuto Cellini (1838), *Les Troyens* (Part 2, 1863/Parts 1 and 2, 1890), *Béatrice et Bénédict* (1862)
Bizet, Georges (1838–75)
 Les Pêcheurs de Perles (1863), *Carmen* (1875)
Boito, Arrigo (1842–1918)
 Mefistofele (1868)
Borodin, Alexander (1833–87)
 Prince Igor (produced 1890)
Britten, Benjamin (1913–76)
 Peter Grimes (1945), *The Rape of Lucretia* (1946), *Albert Herring* (1947), *Let's Make an Opera* (1949), *Billy Budd* (1951), *Gloriana* (1953), *The Turn of the Screw* (1954), *Noyes Fludde* (1958), *A Midsummer Night's Dream* (1960), *Owen Wingrave* (1971),

Death in Venice (1973)
Catalani, Alfredo (1854–93)
 La Wally (1892)
Cavalli, Pier (1602–76)
 L'Ormindo (1644), *Calisto* (1651)
Charpentier, Gustave (1860–1956)
 Louise (1900)
Cherubini, Luigi (1760–1842)
 Médée (1797)
Cilèa, Francesco (1866–1950)
 Adriana Lecouvreur (1902)
Cimarosa, Domenico (1749–1801)
 Il Matrimonio Segreto (1792)
Cornelius, Peter (1824–74)
 Der Barbier von Bagdad (1858)
Dallapiccola, Luigi (1904–75)
 Il Prigioniero (1950)
Debussy, Claude (1862–1918)

Pelléas et Mélisande (1902)
Delibes, Léo (1836–91)
    Lakmé (1883)
Donizetti, Gaetano (1797–1848)
    Anna Bolena (1830), *L'Élisir
    d'Amore* (1832), *Lucia di
    Lammermoor* (1835), *Maria
    Stuarda* (1835), *La Fille du
    Régiment* (1840), *La Favorite*
    (1840), *Don Pasquale* (1843).
Dvořák, Anton (1841–1904)
    Rusalka (1901)
Falla, Manuel de (1876–1946)
    La Vida Breve (1905)
Gershwin, George (1898–1937)
    Porgy and Bess (1935)
Giordano, Umberto (1867–1948)
    Andrea Chénier (1896)
Glinka, Mikhail (1804–57)
    A Life for the Tsar/Ivan Susanin
    (1834–6), *Ruslan and Ludmila*
    (1838–41)
Gluck, Christoph (1714–87)
    Orfeo ed Euridice (1762), *Alceste*
    (1767), *Iphigénie en Aulide* (1773),
    Armide (1777), *Iphigénie en
    Tauride* (1779)
Gounod, Charles (1818–93)
    Faust (1859), *Roméo et Juliette*
    (1867)
Handel, George Frederick (1685–1759)
    Acis and Galatea (1720?), *Alcina*
    (1735), *Serse* (1738), *Samson*
    (1743, staged oratorio), *Semele*
    (1744, staged oratorio)
Haydn, Joseph (1732–1809)
    Il Mondo della Luna (1777)
Henze, Hans Werner (1926–   )
    Boulevard Solitude (1952), *Das
    König Hirsch* (1956), *Der Prinz von
    Homburg* (1960), *Elegy for Young
    Lovers* (1961), *The Bassarids*
    (1966), *We Come to the River* (1976)
Hindemith, Paul (1895–1963)
    Mathis de Maler (1938)
Honegger, Arthur (1892–1955)
    Jeanne d'Arc au Búcher (1936)
Humperdinck, Engelbert (1854–1921)
    Hänsel und Gretel (1893)
Janáček, Leos (1854–1928)
    Jenufa (1904), *Katya Kabanova*
    (1921), *The Cunning Little Vixen*
    (1924), *The Makropoulos Case*
    (1926), *From the House of the
    Dead* (1930)
Kodály, Zoltán (1882–1967)
    Háry János (1926)
Lehár, Franz (1870–1948)
    Die lustige Witwe (1905), *Der Graf
    von Luxembourg* (1909), *Das Land
    des Lächelns* (1929)
Leoncavallo, Ruggiero (1858–1919)

Pagliacci (1892), *La Bohème*
(1897), *Zaza* (1900)
Lortzing, Albert (1801–51)
    Zar und Zimmermann (1837), *Der
    Wildschütz* (1842)
Mascagni, Pietro (1863–1945)
    Cavalleria Rusticana (1890),
    L'Amico Fritz (1891), *Iris* (1898)
Massenet, Jules (1842–1912)
    Hérodiade (1881), *Manon* (1884),
    Werther (1892), *Thaïs* (1894), *Le
    Jongleur de Notre-Dame* (1902),
    Don Quichotte (1910)
Menotti, Gian-Carlo (1911–   )
    The Medium (1946), *The
    Telephone* (1947), *The Consul*
    (1950), *Amahl and the Night
    Visitors* (1951)
Messager, André (1853–1929)
    Véronique (1898), *Monsieur
    Beaucaire* (1919)
Meyerbeer, Giacomo (1791–1864)
    Robert le Diable (1831), *Les
    Huguenots* (1836), *Le Prophète*
    (1849), *L'Africaine* (1865)
Milhaud, Darius (1892–1974)
    Christophe Colomb (1930), *David*
    (1954)
Millöcker, Karl (1842–99)
    Der Bettelstudent (1882)
Moniuszko, Stanislaw (1819–72)
    Halka (1848)
Monteverdi, Claudio (1567?–1643)
    La Favola d'Orfeo (1607), *Il
    Ritorno d'Ulisse in Patria* (1641),
    L'Incoronazione di Poppea (1642)
Mozart, Wolfgang Amadeus (1756–91)
    Idomeneo (1781), *Die Entführung
    aus dem Serail* (1782), *Der
    Schauspieldirektor* (1786), *Le Nozze
    di Figaro* (1786), *Don Giovanni*
    (1787), *Così fan tutte* (1790), *Die
    Zauberflöte* (1791), *La Clemenza di
    Tito* (1791)
Mussorgsky, Modest (1839–81)
    Boris Godunov (1873/4),
    Khovanshschina (post 1886),
    Sorochintsy Fair (unfinished,
    produced 1913)
Nicolai, Otto (1819–49)
    Die lustigen Weiber von Windsor
    (1849)
Offenbach, Jacques (1819–80)
    Orphée aux Enfers (1858), *La Belle
    Hélène* (1864), *La Vie Parisienne*
    (1866), *La Grande Duchesse de
    Gérolstein* (1867), *La Périchole*
    (1868), *Les Contes d'Hoffmann*
    (post 1881)
Orff, Carl (1895–1982)
    Carmina Burana (1937), *Der
    Mond* (1939), *Die Kluge* (1943)

Pfitzner, Hans (1869–1949)
    Palestrina (1917)
Pizzetti, Ildebrando (1880–1968)
    Debora e Jaele (1922), *La Figlia di
    Jorio* (1954), *L'Assassino nella
    Cattedrale* (1958)
Planquette, Robert (1848–1903)
    Les Cloches de Corneville (1877)
Ponchielli, Amilcare (1834–86)
    La Gioconda (1876)
Prokofiev, Serge (1891–1953)
    The Love for Three Oranges
    (1921), *War and Peace* (produced
    1946), *The Fiery Angel* (produced
    1955)
Puccini, Giacomo (1858–1924)
    Manon Lescaut (1893), *La Bohème*
    (1896), *Tosca* (1900), *Madama
    Butterfly* (1904), *La Fanciulla del
    West* (1910), *La Rondine* (1917), *Il
    Trittico* (1918), *Turandot* (post.
    1926)
Purcell, Henry (c. 1659–95)
    Dido and Aeneas (?1689)
Rameau, Jean-Philippe (1683–1764)
    Les Indes Galantes (1735)
Ravel, Maurice (1875–1937)
    L'Heure Espagnole (1907),
    L'Enfant et les Sortilèges (1925)
Reznicek, Emil (1860–1945)
    Donna Diana (1894)
Rimsky-Korsakov, Nikolay (1844–1904)
    The Snow Maiden (1882), *Sadko*
    (1898), *The Golden Cockerel* (1909)
Rossini, Gioacchino (1792–1868)
    Tancredi (1813), *L'Italiana in
    Algeri* (1813), *Il Barbiere di
    Siviglia* (1816), *La Cenerentola*
    (1817), *La Gazza Ladra* (1817),
    Mosè in Egitto (1818, as *Moïse*,
    1827), *Semiramide* (1823), *Le
    Comte Ory* (1823), *Guillaume Tell*
    (1829)
Saint-Saëns, Camille (1835–1921)
    Samson et Dalila (1877)
Schoenberg, Arnold (1874–1951)
    Erwartung (1909, produced 1924),
    Moses und Aron (unfinished,
    produced 1957)
Shostakovich, Dmitri (1906–75)
    *Lady Macbeth of Mtsensk
    (Katerina Ismailova)* (1934)
Smetana, Bedřich (1824–84)
    The Bartered Bride (1866), *Dalibor*
    (1868), *The Two Widows* (1874),
    The Secret (1878)
Spontini, Gasparo (1774–1851)
    La Vestale (1807)
Strauss, Johann (II) (1825–99)
    Die Fledermaus (1874), *Eine Nacht
    in Venedig* (1884), *Der
    Zigeunerbaron* (1885)

Strauss, Richard (1864–1949)
  Salome (1905), *Elektra* (1909), *Der Rosenkavalier* (1911), *Ariadne auf Naxos* (1st version, 1912; 2nd 1916), *Die Frau ohne Schatten* (1919), *Intermezzo* (1924), *Arabella* (1933), *Die schweigsame Frau* (1935), *Capriccio* (1942)
Stravinsky, Igor (1882–1971)
  The Nightingale (1914), *Oedipus Rex* (1927), *The Rake's Progress* (1951)
Sullivan, Arthur (1842–1900)
  From *Trial by Jury* (1875): there are too many of equal merit to list here.
Tchaikovsky, Pyotr (1840–93)
  Eugene Onegin (1879), *The Queen of Spades* (1890)
Thomas, Ambroise (1811–96)

Mignon (1866)
Tippett, Michael (1905–   )
  The Midsummer Marriage (1955), *King Priam* (1962), *The Knot Garden* (1970), *The Ice Break* (1977)
Vaughan Williams, Ralph (1872–1958)
  Hugh the Drover (1924), *Riders to the Sea* (1937)
Verdi, Giuseppe (1813–1901)
  Nabucco (1842), *I Lombardi* (1843), *Ernani* (1844), *I Due Foscari* (1844), *Attila* (1846), *Macbeth* (1847, revised 1865), *La Battaglia di Legnano* (1849), *Luisa Miller* (1849), *Rigoletto* (1851), *Il Trovatore* (1853), *La Traviata* (1853), *Les Vêpres Siciliennes* (1855), *Simon Boccanegra* (1857, revised 1881), *Un Ballo in Maschera* (1859), *La Forza del*

Destino (1862), *Don Carlos* (1867), *Aida* (1871), *Otello* (1887), *Falstaff* (1893)
Wagner, Richard (1813–1883)
  Der fliegende Holländer (1843), *Tannhäuser* (1845, revised 1861), *Lohengrin* (1850), *Tristan und Isolde* (1865), *Die Meistersinger* (1868), *Das Rheingold* (1869), *Die Walküre* (1870), *Siegfried* (1876), *Die Götterdämmerung* (1876), *Parsifal* (1882)
Weber, Carl Maria von (1786–1826)
  Der Freischütz (1821)
Weill, Kurt (1900–50)
  Die Dreigroschenoper (1928), *Mahagonny* (1930)
Wolf-Ferrari, Ermanno (1876–1948)
  I Quatro Rusteghi (1906), *Il Segreto di Susanna* (1909)

Bibliography

The author wishes particularly to acknowledge the ultimate mother-lode of operatic performances since 1950, the back numbers of *Opera* magazine; the various editions of *Kobbé's Complete Opera Book*, now in the care of The Earl of Harewood (latest edition, The Bodley Head, 1987), and the *Concise Oxford Dictionary of Opera* (several editions since 1964, Oxford University Press). The following books in their different ways give an informed and readable glimpse of the world of opera, past and present, though they represent a mere fraction of what is available.

ARUNDELL, DENNIS. *The Story of Sadler's Wells* (Hamish Hamilton, 1965)
BEECHAM, SIR THOMAS. *A Mingled Chime* (Hutchinson, 1944)
BING, RUDOLF. *5000 Nights at the Opera* (Hamish Hamilton, 1972)
BLOM, ERIC (Editor). *Mozart's Letters* (Penguin Books, 1956)
CAIRNS, DAVID (Editor). *The Memoirs of Hector Berlioz* (Gollancz, 1969)
CARNER, MOSCO. *Puccini* (Duckworth, 1958)
GOBBI, TITO. *My Life* (Macdonald and Jane's, 1979)
HUGHES, SPIKE. *Glyndebourne* (Methuen, 1965)
MANN, WILLIAM. *Richard Strauss* (Oxford University Press, 1964)
NEWMAN, ERNEST. *The Life of Richard Wagner*, Vols I–IV (Cassell, 1933–47)
OSBORNE, CHARLES. *The Dictionary of Opera* (Macdonald, 1983)
ROSENTHAL, HAROLD. *My Mad World of Opera* (Weidenfeld & Nicolson, 1982)
STEANE, J.B. *The Grand Tradition* (Duckworth, 1974)
WALKER, FRANK. *The Man Verdi* (Dent, 1962)
WESTERMAN, GERHART VON (Editor, Harold Rosenthal). *Opera Guide* (Thames & Hudson, 1964)

Index